SPICY

Dares & Desires

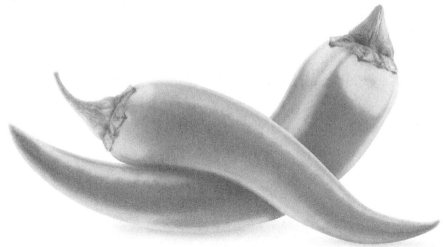

Naughty Truth or Dare
Games for Couples

Cover Design: M Kortekaas

More Frisky Ideas & Games

We hope you're always on the look out for more ways to enhance your relationship and spice up your love life. We believe a vibrant sex life is essential to maintaining a healthy and happy relationship. It's also a vital aspect of your personal well being. The shared intimacy and pleasures of lovemaking is something we all need. But we also crave passion and excitement to keep us feeling more alive. Satisfy your desires by continuing to learn about and experiment with creative ways to make sex thrilling together. Challenge each other to step out of your sexual comfort zone and explore your full erotic potential.

Check out our other books available on Amazon:

- 469 Fun Sex Questions for Couples
- 123 Frisky Sexual Fantasies & Erotic Roleplay Ideas
- Sex Games & Foreplay Ideas for Couples
- Extra Naughty Frisky Foreplay Hot Sex Dice Games

If you have an iPhone or iPad, check out our creative sex apps currently available in the App Store. Just do a search for:

- iLoveRandomSex
- Succulent Expressions
- Sex Questions 42
- Frisky Foreplay
- Spicy Dares & Desires

Play Safe

Safety, mutual respect and trust are essential in any sexual relationship. These elements are required for all intimate love play. The Spicy Dares & Desires foreplay game provides a source of inspiration for new and more exciting sexual activities. It is intended only for consenting adult couples. Various combinations of sex related ideas are presented to stimulate your creative imagination and spark your desire for hot new sensual experiences. All suggestions and activities inspired by the content are strictly voluntary and should be performed at your own risk and discretion. Never coerce your partner to play a role or perform an activity that does not appeal to them. You should also avoid any position, activity or product which is not suitable to your physical or sexual limitations. If there is any uncertainty or doubt, discuss the ideas together with your partner. For additional information, please also refer to the many excellent books on human sexuality available in libraries and bookstores in your area.

Safe Adult Play

Special Note: always clean before inter-mixing anal then vaginal activities to avoid bacterial infections. Use a dental dam for oral-anal activities. Also, avoid getting anything with sugar in the vagina. This can lead to a nasty yeast infection. And, when playing with hot wax, only use low-temperature melting point candles designed for this erotic purpose.

How to Play

You'll need three different colored dice (say red, white, blue). The ordered sequence is used to look up a question or dare. The Red die indicates a max intensity level. The Red/White combo maps to separate Truth and Dare pages. The Blue die points to a specific activity in one of two sections per page. First player to 10 points wins.

Start at level 1 and increase when rolling a triple of the next level (2,2,2 begins level 2). Choose a starting player, then:

- Player decides Truth or Dare, then rolls all three dice.

- If not starting a new level and the Red die is greater than the current level, adjust it down to any *valid* value.

- Use the dice values to lookup an activity in either the top or bottom section as indicated.

- Read the activity to yourself first. <Words> indicate you need to fill in your own. For activities with word lists, attempt to use as many as you can. If desired, adjust or reword items, then read your version aloud to your partner.

- If you rolled a Red/White double, look up a Double Dirty Dare prompt (near the back of the book). Use the dirty words and phrases to make up a dare.

Gain points whenever:

- You roll a level increase triple

- The other player forfeits or fails to perform the activity (take shot optional)

- The other player forfeits or fails to make up a Double Dirty Dare

- The other player declines to participate in a dare you're performing for them

All players should strip an item of clothing whenever the level increases. Higher intensity dares require certain levels of nudity to perform. If it can't be done yet, award a point.

Note: You may randomly hit the same activity multiple times. In this situation, attempt to rephrase, perform, or answer it slightly different each time. Substitute Truth and Dare template pages are included to add in your own activities. Just flag a default item in some way to indicate an alternate is available for that die combo. Fill in the dots on the blank die to indicate specific values.

Also, check out the **Fooling Around** game included at the back of the book.

Female Reads Question

  Frisky Foreplay Feels Fantastic

 Would you consider yourself more of an exhibitionist or voyeur, and why?

 What one part of my body do you find most Suckable?

 What benefits do you think couples can get from watching porn together?

 Have you ever been so overwhelmed with emotions after an intense orgasm that you felt like crying?

 Have you ever performed or received a rim job?

 While shopping in a sex toy store, have you ever bought more than one sex toy at one time?

Male Reads Question

 How many insertable vibrators do you have for penetration?

 Have you ever used a male strap-on in your sex play?

 What different touching techniques would you like to try?

 Have you ever had a boudoir photo or painting made?

 What is the most contorted or acrobatic sex position you have ever tried, and would you consider doing it again?

 At what age did you first use a sex toy?

Female Reads Dare

  Sexy Smart Is Seductive

 Allow me to give you a sensual, fingertip scalp massage.

 Suppose you are a high end-escort on a weekend-long event with a wealthy client. Describe in detail what you would provide for your fee of $25,000.

 Allow me to demonstrate some bondage skills by restraining only your legs. (use rope, tape, cuffs, etc.) Remain bound until your next turn. (The release must be quick and easy to perform.)

 Get into a doggie style position with me and grind against me.

 Delicately stroke my hands and fingers with your fingertips. Swirl and circle as you explore and tickle every nerve to attention.

 Go into the kitchen, find any two items, then describe how you would use them to stimulate yourself.

Male Reads Dare

 Search the internet and find a short porn video involving gay sex and watch it with me.

 Make up a short sexy marketing phrase or expression to advertise your members only Sex Dungeon using the following words: REMOVE TIMER CORONA LOWER BITER PUSSYPUNISHING

 Fondle, Rub and Massage my buttocks.

 While standing together, softly stroke and caress my entire body. Lightly squeeze parts of my body that you find delightful.

 Make up and tell an erotic story that involves me and a police officer. Include appropriately explicit details.

 Make up a short sexy marketing phrase or expression to advertise your members only Sex Dungeon using the following words: MADEOUT BREASTBONDAGE WRITE BLONDEWIG SOUR CREASE

 What is the most extremely thrilling location you can imagine having sex?

 Have you ever made and used an ice dildo? If not, would you like to make one using a condom and toilet paper roll, then try it?

 In a dominant/submissive type fantasy or roleplaying scenario, would you rather be the A: Master/Mistress or B: slave?

 Of all the possible rear entry variations you can imagine, which one do you prefer as the most thrilling?

 What part of your body would you most like me to massage with warm oil right now?

 Who's sex diary would you most like to read, assuming they have one?

Male Reads Question

 What position do you prefer or find most comfortable for receiving oral sex?

 Have you ever made a mess on the bed while having anal sex?

 In what ways do you think couples can use their cell phones to get each other both excited and ready for hot sex together?

 Have you ever played any strip games like strip poker with a group of people?

 How do you most like to prepare for a hot date that you are confident will lead to sex?

 What tips or techniques do you feel people need to learn more about kissing?

Female Reads Dare

Dirty Words Lead To Dirty Deeds

 Tell a sexy story (real or made up) with explicit details that involves: A Male Masturbation Sleeve.

 Describe a possible erotic fantasy using the following words: WAND BENDOVERBUD TUSH PUCKER WET WANG

 Using your tongue, stroke out a single dirty word anywhere on my body with exposed skin until I can guess what it is or time runs out.

 Using all the letters in your first name, create a sex-related acronym or list of erotic ideas, with each one starting with a corresponding letter.

 Describe in detail a fantasy scenario that involves you and me having a quickie in an unusual location.

 Experiment on me with different types of kisses and kissing sensations. (upside down, open mouth, closed mouth, sideways, corner, firm, soft)

Male Reads Dare

 Tell a sexy story (real or made up) with explicit details that involves: A Metal Dildo.

 Pretend to be a horny puppy and hump my leg.

 In a dominant voice, command me to lick and suck a part of your body. Direct exactly how you want it done.

 Remove one article of clothing erotically, then slowly remove one item of clothing from me.

 Use your fingertips to hunt for sensual regions on my back while I am lying face down. Move or adjust any clothing required to make my spine tingle with pleasure.

 Get on your hands and knees in a doggy style position and smack your butt seductively.

Female Reads Question

 Have you ever had or given someone a vampire kiss or hickey?

 Either alone or with a partner, have you ever used, or would you like to try using butt plugs?

 On average, how long do you feel a good lovemaking session should last?

 In what ways do you think couples can use hot erotic talk to get each other more excited?

 When was the last time you remember having a wet dream?

 Have you ever purposely tried to make your sex play as loud as possible?

Male Reads Question

 Have you ever been to a fantasy or erotic roleplaying costume party, and if so, what did you go as?

 What do you believe are the secrets to more and better female orgasms?

 On average, how often do you masturbate? (never, rarely, yearly, monthly, weekly, daily)

 If you could safely skinny dip anywhere in the world and get away with it, where would you most want to do it?

 Have you ever been to a nudist resort?

 How much and what kinds of foreplay do you feel is best before sexual intercourse?

Gently kiss and lick my inner arm – wrist to elbow.

 Make up and tell an erotic story that involves a motorcycle gang and me. Include appropriately explicit details.

 Position me any way you desire, then move in for a creative kiss but freeze just before your lips touch me. Stay as close as possible for 60 seconds, then finish the kiss.

 Find a dildo or other suitable phallic object. I'll hold it between my legs while you demonstrate a sensual "foot job" with bare feet. Use lube or vegetable oil if desired.

 Tell a sexy story (real or made up) with explicit details that involves: A Dual Action Vibrator.

 Make up and tell an erotic story that involves me in a BDSM scenario. Include appropriately explicit details.

Male Reads Dare

 Take me to any location in the home that you haven't had sex in yet. Make me smile by whispering what you could do with me there.

 Starting at my lips, kiss your way down (over clothing if necessary) to a part of my body that you would love to orally pleasure for more than just a few seconds.

 While standing face to face with our eyes closed, delicately caress my face. Trace your fingertips as lightly as you can as you explore every detail.

 We'll both remove one article of clothing and dance close to one slow song. You pick the music.

 I will pretend to be a statue and attempt to remain still for one minute. Use only your lips and tongue to bring me to life. (no biting)

 Describe the features of a innovative stimulation device using the following words for inspiration: NIPPLEJEWELRY STRAPON PRICK BORE ROUSING GLOW

Using the following words for inspiration, what type of sex-related trophy can you imagine being awarded to yourself? NEVER PUMP DOUBLEDONG MUSIC SMOOTH BREASTS

 Suppose you could live a thousand youthful years with futuristic medical advances and capabilities. Do you think you would ever want to experience one or more standard lifetimes as the opposite gender?

 Have you ever had, or would you like to have, sex in a cave?

 In your favorite erotic stories or fantasies, what types of settings, roles or activities turn you on the most?

 Using the following words for inspiration, what erotic activity can you imagine <insert couple> doing together? SECRET BUBBLES SPLASH BREASTBONDAGE BODY INTIMATE

 Have you ever played with yourself to show a lover how you like it?

Male Reads Question

 What is your most memorable experience with a past lover?

 Which sex positions do you find most stimulating?

 What is one of your unusual quirks (in or out of the bedroom) that makes you adorable?

 What color of lipstick do you think is the most erotic when performing, receiving or watching a blow job?

 What forms of nipple stimulation do you enjoy receiving most?

 In a "forced sex" fantasy or roleplaying scenario, would you rather be A: the intruder or B: the resident?

Go to the kitchen and find something edible that's liquid. While I am bent over slightly, dribble some on my neck, so it runs down my back. Then lick it up. Move or adjust clothing as required.

 Make up and tell an erotic story that involves me and a dark ritual. Include appropriately explicit details.

 Seductively crawl around on the floor like a cat on the prowl or one looking for affection. Purr with love or growl with lust.

 Describe in detail a fantasy scenario that involves you and me having a quickie outside (moonlit night, beach, parked car, under a bridge, etc.).

 Tell a sexy story (real or made up) with explicit details that involves: An Extra Large Dildo.

 Demonstrate your bondage skills by restraining only my legs. (use rope, tape, cuffs, etc.) I will remain bound until after the next turn. (The release must be quick and easy to perform.)

Male Reads Dare

 Massage one part of my body (my choice). Experiment with a different type of technique.

 Using only your lips, tongue and teeth, tease your way from my wrist all the way to my ear.

 Use a dildo and some lube to demonstrate how you would give me a creative hand job.

 Go to the kitchen and find something edible that is gooey, sticky or creamy. I'll smear some on one of my fingers for you to lick or suck off.

 Get into a position with me where our butts are cheek to cheek. Erotically massage my butt with yours by wiggling and grinding against it.

 Tell a sexy story (real or made up) with explicit details that involves: A Toy With Beads or Balls.

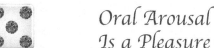

 Using the following words for inspiration, what sex tips come to mind? BAG HUSBAND VIXEN SHAVING OYSTER LEWD

 What one part of my body do you find most Arousing?

 When it comes to playful activities for couples to keep their relationship fun and exciting, how do you think people can come up with more new ideas to try?

 Using the following words for inspiration, what erotic novel title comes to mind? GUSH THUMB TATTOO EVIL QUIM <BodyPart>

 What type of words or sounds help push you over the edge when nearing climax?

 Either alone or with a partner, have you ever used, or would you like to try using anal dildos?

Male Reads Question

 Have you ever had sex outside in the snow?

 What is your idea of a romantic vacation or weekend getaway?

 What do you consider the best position to avoid premature ejaculation?

 Have you ever done a 69 position standing or sitting up? Would you like to try doing it?

 Would you cross-dress for a roleplaying scenario?

 Have you ever had sex without any kissing?

Whisper something hot and dirty in my ear that you're sure will make me smile with wicked excitement.

 Get on one knee and give me a pretend marriage proposal. Make it is sound as sincere as possible.

 Tell a sexy story (real or made up) with explicit details that involves: A Flavored Love Oil or Lube.

 Sit across from me and pretend we're at a restaurant with the table cloth covering our laps. Using your feet, attempt to pleasure me as surreptitiously as possible.

 Write down a sexy challenge for me to perform sometime later this week. It must be a safe, fun and plausible activity that will be enjoyable to all involved.

 Put an edible topping or liquor in your navel and entice me to lick it out.

Male Reads Dare

 Simulate a sex act of your choice without involving me – I get to watch as you pretend. Stimulate my desire.

 Suppose we were going to explore "furry play" together. Describe the animal costumes you would want each of us to wear and what we would do.

 Drag your fingernails down my back, chest and tummy, legs or arms - your choice.

 Describe a possible self pleasuring activity using the following words: CHILLIPEPPERS BACKDOOR WETTER ENOUGH OBSERVE FOOT

 Perform a back of knee tongue tickle on me.

 Sit across from me and pretend we're at a restaurant with the table cloth covering our laps. Using your feet, attempt to pleasure me as surreptitiously as possible.

Female Reads Question

 Which sex positions do you find most comfortable?

 How do you most enjoy being touched during foreplay?

 Do you usually masturbate with sex toys?

 Would you rather have me roleplay as a sexy yet innocent angel or a hot and naughty devil?

 Do you prefer playing with hard or soft dildos?

 Have you ever used, or would you like to try using clit clips?

Male Reads Question

 Have you ever had, or would you like to have, sex in a tropical jungle?

 Imagine that you gained the secret power to transform into the opposite sex and back again, but no one else would ever know. Would you want to experiment with gay or lesbian sex?

 Have you ever had, or would you like to have, sex on a mountain?

 In a fantasy or roleplaying scenario set in ancient times, would you rather be the traveler or native?

 In a dominant/submissive type fantasy or roleplaying scenario, would you rather be the A: pimp or B: prostitute?

 What type of reading material turns you on the most?

Female Reads Dare

  Dirty Words Lead To Dirty Deeds

 Tell a sexy story (real or made up) with explicit details that involves: A Wearable Vibrator.

 Find some high heels that might fit and try to walk in them. Wear them for as long as you can during the rest of the game.

 Describe a creepy yet erotic mask you might try wearing for "fun sex".

 Suppose we were going to explore a gender swap roleplay scenario. Describe in detail what kinds of sex play activities we would try out.

 Give feather-light kisses along my neck and jawline. Breathe softly next to my ear to make me shiver with delight.

 Pretend to be a statue. See if you can remain still for one minute while I use only my lips and tongue to bring you to life. (no biting)

Male Reads Dare

 Perform a ballroom dance with a pretend or ghost partner.

 Using all the letters in my first name, create a sex-related acronym or list of erotic ideas, with each one starting with a corresponding letter.

 Give me a sexy and sincere compliment.

 Pretend you're a high fashion model. Strut your stuff with flair as if you were walking down a catwalk.

 Massage my feet and each toe with massage oil or lube.

 Make up and tell an erotic story that involves me and a "deflowering" scenario. Include appropriately explicit details.

For someone of the opposite sex you find attractive, how would you describe the perfect legs?

 What is the best dirty joke that you can remember?

 Using the following words for inspiration, what fantasy scenario comes to mind? FIND RIM STRAWBERRIES EAGER SISSY SQUIRTPAD

 Using the following words for inspiration, what sex tips come to mind? DANCING ARMPITHAIR SISSY BUTTPLUG FLUFFER ENORMOUS

 What flavor of lube would you use for rimming?

 What websites do you use to search for, research and/or buy sex toys?

Male Reads Question

 While shopping in a sex toy store, have you ever squeezed a realistic dildo to feel it's texture and shape?

 If you were commissioned to create an instructional sex video on one topic, what would it be about?

 In a "forced sex" fantasy or roleplaying scenario, would you rather be A: the conquerer or B: the conquered?

 Of the sexual features you've ever seen personally on a man, how saggy was the saggiest sack?

 Have you ever used a double dildo together with a lover for mutual anal pleasure?

 Using the following words for inspiration, what type of sex-related trophy can you imagine being awarded to me? FOXTAILPLUG SHAG HEADPHONES FIRM SPOT MUFF

On a single sheet of blank paper, draw the life-sized shape of a custom-designed dildo for use in your sex play.

 Describe in explicit detail a fantasy scenario with me that involves role reversal or gender play.

 Suppose you were about to list yourself on a sex-for-money site. Quickly write/ draw a short ad describing your unique services, then reveal it.

 Stroke and caress my legs and inner thighs.

 Put on a pair of nylons or sexy woman's stockings and keep them on during the game as an item of clothing.

 Expose your butt and put on a sexy show by making it move in the most erotic way you can think of.

Male Reads Dare

 Create a list of "sexual firsts" that you have never done but want to try at least once.

 Pretend to be a very affectionate cat eager to get my attention.

 Make up and tell an erotic story that involves me and a castle. Include appropriately explicit details.

 Hold an ice cube between your lips and use it to stimulate an exposed region on my body.

 Use a digital camera and play erotic photographer with me. We'll review them together and delete afterward (unless you really like one to print).

 Stroke my tail bone and between my butt cheeks. Use your fingers, tongue, feather, spoon, a string of beads, etc.

 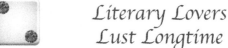
Female Reads Question

 What forms of sex education did you receive, and how are you continuing to learn more?

 Which sex positions do you find most intimate?

 Have you fantasized about "other people" while masturbating or having sex?

 What sex position creates the most intense type of orgasm for you?

 Have you ever licked and sucked a lover's toes or had your toes licked and sucked on?

 Were there any school teachers that you had a secret crush on or fantasized about having sex with?

Male Reads Question

 If you were going to play as my love pet, what type of animal would you want to be?

 When it comes to naughty playthings, have you ever been caught masturbating with toys?

 In a dominant/submissive type fantasy or roleplaying scenario, would you rather be the A: teacher or B: student?

 Using the following words for inspiration, what new oral pleasuring ideas come to mind? ANALLY PUSH VAGINA ROCK RIGHT SUBMISSIVES

 How do you feel about playful scratching during foreplay or while having sex?

 When it comes to playfully romantic, sexy or erotic activities to enjoy, where do you get your best ideas?

 While I sit, perform a lap dance for me to one song of your choice. Seductively rub and grind yourself on me.

 Make up short sexy phrase or expression for an erotic award, certificate or trophy using the following words: FEMINIZATION PEEK BREATHLESS LIQUOR SIMULTANEOUS EYEBROW

 Give me a sensual hand massage using oil or lube.

 Using the following words for inspiration, describe a scenario that involves amazing oral delights: SYRUP SEDUCTIVELY BITEME ENGORGE LAP BOOTWORSHIP

 Pretend you're an erotic cheerleader inspiring a couple making love. Make up and perform a sexy cheer.

 Pretend you are performing oral sex on a ghost pussy that only you can see and feel.

Male Reads Dare

 Describe a BDSM accessory you would like to try out with me. Include explicit details on how it would be used.

 Find a free porn site on the internet and watch a short video on mute. Do a voice over for the action while I provide a supporting role.

 Lightly drag your fingernails down my back while I stand in front of you. Move or adjust any clothing required to make my spine tingle with pleasure.

 Tell a sexy story (real or made up) with explicit details that involves: A Leather Collar.

 Suppose you're pitching the design of a life-size, realistic silicone replica of my butt for a line of sex toys. Sell my ass as best as you can to a pretend design team.

 Make up a short sexy blurb for an extra kinky novel pitch using the following words: GYRATE THRUSTS WOOD THIGH CUFFED BULLRING

Female Reads Question

 What creatively sensual activities can you imagine doing to each other with whipped cream?

 What are your favorite sex toys for masturbation?

 What is the strangest name you have ever heard for a sex position or activity?

 What is the fastest time you can remember that you made yourself orgasm masturbating?

 Have you ever had, or would you like to have, sex in a lush forest?

 How would you feel about being blindfolded while I surprise you with pleasure?

Male Reads Question

 Have you ever used a glass or steel butt plug?

 What is the fastest time you can remember that a partner orgasmed when having sex with you?

 Have you ever had sex with other people watching? Was it done on purpose, or did it just happen?

 On what days and times of day do you most feel like enjoying more sensual foreplay?

 Have you ever used a vibrator in a semi-public location with people close by?

 Have you ever had, or would you like to have, sex in a blooming orchard?

Put an edible topping or liquor in my navel and lick it out.

 Make up and tell an erotic story that involves me in an anonymous sex scenario. Include appropriately explicit details.

 Describe an elegant and erotic mask you might try wearing if you were having or roleplaying a mysteriously romantic affair.

 Make up a short sexy blurb for an erotic movie pitch using the following words: SERVE CANAL LIMBER THORN WETDREAM MADAME

 Make up short sexy phrase or expression for an erotic award, certificate or trophy using the following words: DININGROOM SPERM SEEP FRICTION HUGEANALDILDO POTENT

 Make up short sexy phrase or expression for an erotic award, certificate or trophy using the following words: SPOON MUSCLE UNTIL STRAPLESSDOUBLEDILDO CANOODLE SOFT

Male Reads Dare

 Make up short sexy phrase or expression for an erotic award, certificate or trophy using the following words: LUBRICATION RAVENOUSLY REACH WIZARD FIND GSPOT

 Slowly and sensually lick and suck my thumb. Stimulate every nerve with your twirling tongue.

 Choose a dildo and place it between your legs. Then, without using your hands, walk at least 10 feet without dropping it.

 Lightly stroke and tease a part of my body as you whisper naughty things that will arouse and excite both of us.

 Tell a sexy story (real or made up) with explicit details that involves: A Clitoral Vibrator.

 Lightly drag your fingernails up then down each of my legs while I stand in front of you. Go overtop of any clothing if required.

Female Reads Question

  *Juicy & Sweet Or Hot & Sour*

 What's the funniest tip you have ever heard or seen in a sex advice article?

 Using the following words for inspiration, what sex related Yes/No questions would you most like to ask me? SPANKING BOUNCE EXOTIC MEAT THIGHHARNESS JUGS

 If you were hypnotized and made to believe that the clitoris and labia tasted like candy when you performed oral sex, what flavor would you prefer?

 In a sci-fi fantasy or roleplaying scenario, would you rather be A: exotic alien or B: human visitor?

 Using the following words for inspiration, what new oral pleasuring ideas come to mind? CLIMAX BLISS DROOP ATHLETE HEELS MANBOOB

 What's the most number of orgasms you remember having in one session of sex?

Male Reads Question

 If I was to play as your love pet, what type of animal would you want me to be?

 What is your favorite technique for achieving a G-Spot orgasm?

 Do you prefer playing with a realistic, penis-shaped dildo or one that does not resemble a real penis?

 Have you ever used a simulated tongue device?

 Can intercourse be part of foreplay?

 What is your best quality out of the bedroom?

Allow me to doll you up with some makeup.

 Massage one part of my body (your choice). Experiment with a different type of technique.

 Let's both sit in a lotus position facing each other. We'll place a hand on each other's chest, close our eyes and synchronize breathing slowly.

 Kiss and nibble along my neck and shoulder.

 Tell a sexy story (real or made up) with explicit details that involves: A Male Strap-on Harness and Dildo.

 Make up short sexy phrase or expression for an erotic award, certificate or trophy using the following words: BACKDOOR SENSITIVE DESERT ROSE INHIBITIONS BOW

Male Reads Dare

 Lightly drag your fingernails down my back, chest and tummy, legs or arms – your choice.

 Say as many euphemisms for anal sex play as you can think of. Make up some if necessary.

 Give me a sensual scalp massage using just your fingertips.

 Make up and tell an erotic story that involves me and a supernatural being. Include appropriately explicit details.

 Whisper something hot and dirty in my ear and see if you can make me blush.

 Suppose we were going to explore a gender swap roleplay scenario. Describe in detail what kinds of sex play activities we would try out.

Female Reads Question

 Have you ever listened to an erotic audio story or guided fantasy?

 In what ways do you think people can make their sex play more creative and erotically adventurous?

 On a hot summer day, have you ever tried spending the day completely naked? Would you like to try it?

 What is your favorite technique for stimulating a G-Spot orgasm?

 What types of things do you do to improve your knowledge about sex?

 How do you feel about your first sexual experiences?

Male Reads Question

 Have you ever enjoyed sex play that involved spanking?

 If you were going to dress me up as a woman, what colors and style of outfit would you choose for me?

 If you were to play out a modern-day fantasy or roleplaying scenario, would you rather be A: a photographer or B: a model?

 In a dominant/submissive type fantasy or roleplaying scenario, would you rather be the A: boss or B: employee?

 Have you ever seen any sex machines in action online or in porn, and if so, which one was the most fascinating?

 Do you prefer to masturbate in the shower/bath or in bed?

Female Reads Dare

 Light a candle and drip some warm, melted wax somewhere on your body. (drip from far enough away to cool a bit and ensure it's not too hot to burn)

 Pretend you can't talk or make any sounds. Using your own unique erotic sign language, attempt to proposition me into performing some form of sexual activity with you.

 Whisper something in my ear that sounds hot and steamy but is in another language. It can be anything as long as you make it sound sultry and sexy.

 Suppose you were about to list yourself on a sex-for-money site. Write down a menu of sexual services on offer with a reasonable/competitive price for each - list at least 5.

 Trace your tongue slowly and sensually all around my lips.

 For the next 60 seconds, allow me to stimulate your nipples using only my fingers. However, no clothing can be moved or removed to gain access to them.

Male Reads Dare

 Describe a possible erotic fantasy using the following words: MILKY LUST OIL PENISENVY AREOLA CUNNILINGUS

 With me laying on the floor passively, get on top and simulate having sex but with you performing all the thrusting or grinding motions.

 Push me up against a wall and kiss me as passionately as you dare.

 Lovingly gaze into my eyes for as long as possible without turning away.

 Make up short sexy phrase or expression for an erotic award, certificate or trophy using the following words: SWORD ROUSING GASP LEATHERCUFF MIRROR WOMAN

 Pretend you're in a confessional. Make up a sexy sin involving you and me that would make the priest want to banish you from the church.

Female Reads Question

 For mysterious reasons, you wake up with a mixture of gender traits. Which combination would you rather have? A: Feminine features including breasts but with a penis and testicles or B: Masculine features but with a vagina and clitoris

 Have you ever had, or would you like to have, sex in a tunnel?

 What kinds of different sex positions or activities can you imagine performing with the use of a hammock?

 Using the following words for inspiration, what roleplay scenario comes to mind? SPEAK THROBBING MANBOOB STROKER OVERFLOW POTION

 What color and style of high heels do you think are the sexiest?

 Of the sexual features you've ever seen personally on a woman, how large was the biggest clitoris?

Male Reads Question

 What do you think BDSM stands for?

 Would you ever consider timing yourself to determine the fastest time to perform oral sex to orgasm?

 What flavor or color of jello would you love to have sex in?

 What is one TV show you remember watching while growing up that has the most erotic potential for roleplaying ideas?

 Have you ever sexually distracted the driver of a moving vehicle either visually or physically?

 What regular item of clothing or fashion accessory do you find most erotic or attractive?

Female Reads Dare

 In one long lick, trace your tongue up my leg along any/all exposed skin from ankle to thigh.

 Tell a sexy story (real or made up) with explicit details that involves: A Female Strap-on Harness and Dildo.

 While standing together, hug and caress me from behind.

 Put a flavored lube or syrup on any rarely licked erogenous zone and entice me to lick it off.

 Tell a sexy story (real or made up) with explicit details that involves: Vibrating Nipple Clips.

 Give me an upside-down kiss as innocent, intimate or passionate as you desire.

Male Reads Dare

 Describe your pussy using 5 words. Use flattering adjectives.

 Tell a sexy story (real or made up) with explicit details that involves: A Double Anal Probe.

 Kiss, lick and suck each finger of my non-dominant hand. Apply a flavored lube or syrup if you desire.

 Change or redress into a sexy roleplaying outfit – slutty vixen, innocent schoolgirl, horny executive, genie, dominatrix – let yourself go wild. Choose something to turn me on.

 Bend over the armrest of a sofa and receive an erotic spanking from me. (bare your butt if desired)

 Straddle the armrest of a chair or sofa and turn yourself on by rubbing and grinding your crotch on it.

Female Reads Question

Be As Naughty
As You Can Be

 Have you ever had, or would you like to have, sex on a dock or pier?

 What kinds of same-sex scenes in fantasy, stories or porn turn you on?

 How curious about sex were you as a kid, and what kinds of things did you do to satisfy your curiosity?

 How many different gay sex positions can you think of in 30 seconds?

 What one part of my body do you find most Attractive?

 What kinds of bondage devices or contraptions would you like to try, and how do you imagine you would use them?

Male Reads Question

 What is the strangest thing that unexpectedly turned you on?

 What do you think is the sexiest sport or competition to either play or watch?

 Using the following words for inspiration, what new oral pleasuring ideas come to mind? STONE SAY HOTWAXPLAY GENITALS BRUTAL MUFF

 If you were to play out a "deflowering" fantasy scenario, how would you feel about roleplaying one with a young virgin initiated by ... (make up the rest of the question)?

 Have you ever had or given someone an electric kiss?

 Using the following words for inspiration, what name for a creative new sex toy comes to mind? RAW BETWEEN PROSTATE NIPPLEPIERCING RIPPEDBLOUSE LINGER

Female Reads Dare

 Make up explicit details for a roleplay scenario based on: She's Sleeping Beauty. He's a prince traveling through the woods, where he finds her alone and vulnerable.

 Take a smartphone with a camera to a semi-private area and take a naked "butt selfie". Edit it as desired, then come back and reveal it. Delete it afterward.

 Make up explicit details for a roleplay scenario based on: She's a border guard. He's a traveler taken aside for random inspection. His suitcase contains some interesting items.

 Have me get into any position you desire. I'll allow you to expose my butt and administer a sensual spanking.

 Describe a Christmas themed roleplay scenario or fantasy that you think I would enjoy.

 Take a smartphone with a video or audio recording feature into another room. Record a short, explicitly dirty LIE about something you could have done in your sexual past, then return and reveal it. Delete it afterward.

Male Reads Dare

 Take a smartphone with a camera to a semi-private area and take a naked ""butt selfie"" after you have self-inserted a butt plug. Edit it as desired, then come back and reveal it. Delete it afterward.

 Come into the bathroom with me and hold my penis while I attempt to pee.

 Demonstrate your favorite oral sex technique using any suitable object or available sex toy.

 Kiss and lick any of my exposed erogenous zones that you desire.

 Suppose you're pitching the design of a life-size, realistic silicone replica of your vulva for a line of sex toys. Sell your pussy as best as you can to a pretend design team.

 Massage my head with the tips of your fingers.

What types of music do you find best for making love?

 Using the following words for inspiration, what masturbation fantasy comes to mind? BONDAGESTOCKADE PAT TRIPOD CUNTS FLOOD GORGEOUS

 What creatively sensual activities can you imagine doing to each other with ice or popsicles?

 What's the most expensive sex toy you own?

 If you were to play out a mythical fantasy or roleplaying scenario, would you rather be the A: angel or B: demon? Describe a sexy situation or storyline you might like to try.

 How many times do you masturbate on average per week?

Male Reads Question

 How much and what types of kissing do you enjoy?

 How can someone learn to be a better kisser?

 Using the following words for inspiration, what erotic activity can you imagine <insert couple> doing together? BEND BLACKLACELINGERIE STANDINGSEX BALL RISQUE BRAZILIAN

 Have you ever masturbated with a butt plug or anal dildo?

 If I was to make you a video of me masturbating, what kinds of things would you like to see me doing in the video? What type of camera angle or shot would you prefer?

 Where and how would you most like to have sex in a semi-public location?

For the next 60 seconds, allow me to stimulate your nipples using only my fingers with massage oil or lube. Clothing can be moved or removed to gain access to them.

 Make up a short sexy Anniversary Card phrase or expression using the following words: SCREAMING SECRETFANTASIES JAWLINE FLOOD GLOVE ADVENTUROUS

 Come into the bathroom with me and watch closely while I attempt to pee.

 Make up and tell an erotic story that involves me in a Victorian-era scenario. Include appropriately explicit details.

 Seductively lick a part of your own body as if you were performing oral sex.

 Describe in detail the most extreme, weird or bizarre sexual activity you can think of doing with or to me (not that you want to do it, of course).

Male Reads Dare

 For the next 60 seconds, expose and stimulate your nipples using your fingers with massage oil or lube.

 Tell a sexy story (real or made up) with explicit details that involves: A Long Slender Dildo.

 Text me a sexy message. Be naughty and make it as hot and dirty as you can.

 Describe in detail a fantasy scenario that involves you and me enjoying a role reversal or gender play activity.

 Suppose you were abducted by aliens. Describe in detail the shape and features of their anal probe that you might actually enjoy.

 Get into a position with me where our butts are cheek to cheek. Wiggle and grind your butt as if we're joined together with a double dildo.

Female Reads Question

 What erotic fantasies, sexy stories or roleplaying scenarios can you think of that would fit the title Up Against the Wall?

 Using the following words for inspiration, what sex-magic spell would you most like to use on anyone? CAMERA HUSBAND FULL BONDAGE HIPS OVERCOME

 Using the following words for inspiration, what futuristic sexual device or sex toy technology comes to mind? LAVA THIGH COAX THORN HOT STILETTOHEELS

 What kinds of sex play activities make you feel delightfully submissive?

 Have you ever put a glass dildo in the freezer before using it?

 When did you lose your virginity, and what was your first time like?

Male Reads Question

 What kinds of stimulating lubricants, oils or creams would you like to try?

 What was your experience like when you first had intercourse?

 Do you like to be spanked as an erotic turn on, or would you prefer to be the one doing the spanking?

 Have you ever masturbated to visually arouse a lover?

 How would you creatively use a butt plug or anal dildo during sex play with me?

 Have you ever used a vibrating butt plug?

Female Reads Dare

 Put on any item to look, feel, smell or taste even more sexy for yourself and me.

 Lightly caress up then down each of my legs while I stand in front of you. Go overtop of any clothing if required.

 Redress into a new piece of visually and sensually erotic clothing that you know will arouse me.

 While you're standing, allow me to lightly drag my nails down your back. Your clothing may be moved or adjusted as required so you can be teased with spine-tingling pleasure.

 Using the following words for inspiration, describe a scenario that involves amazing oral delights: LOTION EROTIC PALM DISCIPLINE DIRTYTALK GROAN

 Allow me to slide my hand up the back of your neck, spread my fingers slightly in your hair and grab a handful. I'll assert a sense of dominance by tugging or pulling your hair with a firm grip. (no hair yanking)

Male Reads Dare

 Choose a dildo and place it between your butt cheeks. Then, without using your hands, walk at least 10 feet without dropping it.

 Find and read out loud to me a how-to article on a sex technique or activity that you have not yet experienced. Scan through a few sex books or search the internet.

 While I'm sitting with feet on the floor, straddle one of my legs, then rub and grind your crotch on my thigh.

 Pretend you are performing oral sex on a ghost cock that only you can see and feel.

 Use your fingers and lube to pleasure me any way you desire.

 Describe in detail a fantasy scenario that involves you and me enjoying a taboo sex play activity.

What kinds of erotica do you enjoy for self-pleasure or masturbation?

 What type of female profession do you feel has the hottest looking style of dress?

 What other types of stimulation do you need during intercourse to increase your ability to orgasm?

 What flavor of jam would make my toes tastier for you?

 Do you know what the sexual term "Fisting" involves? How do you feel about learning more and trying it?

 Are there any types of porn style money shots that you would actually like to experience or perform?

Male Reads Question

 Have you ever had, or would you like to have, sex in a cemetery?

 Have you ever received cunnilingus and discovered it was that time of the month? Would you still consider enjoying oral-clitoral stimulation at this time?

 What is the kinkiest type of foreplay activity that you would like to try?

 What erotic fantasies, sexy stories or roleplaying scenarios can you think of that would fit the title Service With a Smile?

 If you were designing a secret love den, adult playroom or private sex dungeon for two, how would it look, and what would you include in it? Try to describe it in as much detail as you can (style, color, toys, accessories, furniture, etc.).

 What kind of erotic story or fantasy can you think of that is set in a desert oasis?

Female Reads Dare

  Talk Dirty To Me

 Describe, in detail, your favorite or most successful technique for stimulating a G-Spot orgasm.

 Imagine we are roleplaying a gender swap scenario. Pretend I am wearing a strap on and we're going to have intercourse. Choose any position and simulate having sex with me but with you playing the woman.

 Describe in explicit detail what you would do to me if I were tied up naked and spread-eagled on my stomach.

 Suppose you changed into a lesbian female for an hour and could have sex with anyone other than me. Tell me who it would be with and what you would do together. Describe the sex in detail.

 Kneel in front of me and pretend to have a conversation with my pussy. Use a funny voice to speak for my happy hole.

 Take a smartphone with a camera to a semi-private area and take a naked "nipple selfie". Edit it as desired, then come back and reveal it. Delete it afterward.

Male Reads Dare

 Creatively use an ice cube to perk up sensitive regions on my body. Follow each cold shock with a warm kiss or lick.

 Kiss and lick my feet. Suck on my toes.

 While we stand together, let me cup your crotch firmly in one hand with my palm over your clit. Pulse your PC muscles as tightly and quickly as you can for a minute.

 Tell a sexy story (real or made up) with explicit details that involves: A Dildo with a Suction Cup Base.

 Put on a man's dress shirt and tie.

 I'll hold a dildo of your choice while you demonstrate how you would give me a foot job. Use lube if you desire.

Female Reads Question

 What could I do that would make you fantasize all day about having sex with me?

 Of the sexual features you've ever seen personally on a woman, how large was the biggest pair of boobs?

 Have you ever farted while a lover was going down on you?

 In a "forced sex" fantasy or roleplaying scenario, would you rather be A: the prisoner or B: the guard?

 Have you ever used, or would you like to try using a dildo made of Glass?

 What roleplay scenario, fantasy or erotic story can you imagine involving an erotic variation of a fairy tale?

Male Reads Question

 What new anal sex toys would you like to try in your sex play?

 How do you think you could recreate the exciting feelings of your first times having certain types of sexual experiences?

 Would you ever consider timing yourself to determine the fastest time to get into ten sex positions?

 What erotic activity comes to mind when thinking of all these words combined? DUCTTAPE BOOBIES SHOWER FACE FONDLE CELLPHONE

 In your favorite erotic stories or fantasies, do you identify most with the dominant or submissive characters?

 If you were to get lessons from a dominatrix, what kinds of things would you want to learn about?

Make up and tell an erotic story that involves me and a mythical creature. Include appropriately explicit details.

 With you lying on the floor passively, I'll get on top, and we'll simulate having sex together, but with me performing all the thrusting or grinding motions.

 Make up a fantasy scenario or roleplaying adventure for both of us. Include elements of a "real" fantasy to keep me guessing.

 Find a dildo or other suitable phallic object. I'll hold it between my legs while you demonstrate a sensual "hand job" technique. Use lube or vegetable oil if desired.

 Make up and tell an erotic story that involves me and an enchanted sex doll. Include appropriately explicit details.

 Simulate a sex act of your choice as if we both switched gender. I'll use a dildo as a prop if desired.

Male Reads Dare

 Make up explicit details for a roleplay scenario based on: He's a rich and powerful executive. She's a personal assistant looking to get even more personal with him alone in the boardroom.

 Describe in detail how you might like to include a strap-on in a new position or sex play activity with me. If you have one, get it on and let's have a bit of fun.

 Reveal in detail an exotic roleplaying adventure you "may" be interested in experiencing with me. Include explicit content.

 Experience Aural Sex with me. We can call a phone sex line together. Alternatively, we can listen to an erotic CD or porn soundtrack (no watching) together.

 Write a short personal ad as if you were in the market for anonymous sexual partners for quickie hookups. Wildly exaggerate your supposed level of promiscuity with explicit details about the dirty deeds you want to do.

 Simulate a sex act of your choice as if we both switched gender. Use a dildo as a prop if you desire.

Female Reads Question

  Tongue In Cheek Teaser

 What do you feel are the benefits of masturbation?

 What sorts of pain play would you like to experiment with?

 Using the following words for inspiration, what dirty joke comes to mind? STONE EYECONTACT LARGE THRUST RIDEONSEXTOY LIP

 In how many creative ways can you think of using any form of music to enhance our sex play?

 What style or type of dildo would you purchase for me if you got to see me masturbate with it?

 Would you rather be tied up and ravished or blindfolded and sensually surprised?

Male Reads Question

 What do you think is the best sex position and stimulation technique for having vaginal orgasms?

 What types of lingerie do you wear to make yourself feel the most sexy, romantic and in the mood?

 In a dominant/submissive type fantasy or roleplaying scenario, would you rather be A: royalty or B: servant?

 What does it mean to you if a woman "spits or swallows" while giving head?

 If you were magically given the ability to perform any unique erotic trick with any part of your body, what would you want it to be? What power would you choose for me?

 In a sci-fi fantasy or roleplaying scenario, would you rather be A: alien ruler or B: human "god"?

Describe in detail a raunchy S/M or bondage scenario involving you and me.

 Massage my toes one at a time.

 Make up and tell an erotic story that involves me having an affair with a celebrity. Include appropriately explicit details.

 Flicker your tongue along a path entirely around my body, just above the underwear line. Adjust any clothing as required to lick bare skin.

 Give me a sensual neck and shoulder massage.

 Put on high heels if there are any available that fit, and try walking with them.

Male Reads Dare

 Lead me into a dark closet or bathroom for some private, above the belt hanky-panky.

 Suppose we were making and starring in a full-length, start to finish lovemaking movie. Describe in detail what we would do together to make it an exciting film to watch.

 Make up explicit details for a roleplay scenario based on: You're a dominatrix turned pussy cat burglar. She's the wealthy homeowner. You have her tied up trying to make her divulge the combination to her safe.

 Go to the kitchen and find something edible that is gooey, sticky or creamy. Apply it with your finger to an exposed spot on my body, then sensually lick it off.

 Describe in detail a raunchy sex scenario or fantasy involving you and me in a threesome.

 Describe a possible erotic fantasy using the following words: WHITELINGERIE JILLEDOFF BONE SLUTTY SURGE PURRING

Female Reads Question

  Be As Naughty As You Can Be

 Would you ever consider timing yourself to determine the fastest time to finish a hand job?

 If you had to give verbal instructions to someone about to make love for the first time, what would you say to help them perform cunnilingus?

 How long would you say was the longest-lasting orgasm you've ever had?

 Do you prefer to keep your eyes open or closed while kissing or having sex?

 Are there any foreplay skills that you feel you need to learn or relearn?

 Imagine we mind swap with our partner every other time we have sex. We experience sex with their body, then switch back after our orgasms and a nap. How would this affect your desire to try mutual masturbation?

Male Reads Question

 How do you feel about sex play involving erotic spanking, paddles or whips?

 Have you ever dressed in an outfit so that your lover could rip and tear it off of you?

 Have you ever been anally pleasured with a finger, butt plug or anal dildo while receiving or performing a hand job?

 Which sex positions do you find most thrilling?

 Have you ever experienced a blended G-Spot and cunnilingus orgasm? Including female ejaculation?

 What is the most ticklish region on your body, and what kinds of stimulation there drives you crazy?

Female Reads Dare

 Make up explicit details for a roleplay scenario based on: He's the delivery man and she's the eager customer of a sexy new toy.

 Without saying a word, flirtatiously arouse my interest using only your eyes and facial expressions. Make your suggestive desires deliciously hot and steamy.

 Pretend I am an erotic photographer and you're the model. Make some sexy poses as if I was taking pictures for an explicit porn magazine.

 Pretend that you're a doctor and I'm a patient about to be intimately examined by you. Doctor's orders must be followed.

 Go to the kitchen and find something edible that's liquid. Dribble it down my cleavage but lick up every drop before it gets on any article of clothing or reaches my pubic region.

 Spread my butt cheeks wide and tickle my perineum and surrounding erogenous zones with a feather or piece of silky material.

Male Reads Dare

 Make up explicit details for a roleplay scenario based on: She's a tribal warrior woman who captures a missionary worker and decides to corrupt him.

 Use a vibrator to stimulate my neck, chest and nipples.

 Delicately lick around each of my ears. Hot breaths in my ear will give me delightful shivers of pleasure.

 While I stand in front of you, kiss from my ankle up then down each of my legs. Go over the top of any clothing if required.

 Wear a ball gag until the next turn that requires you to remove it in order to play.

 Imagine we are roleplaying a gender swap scenario. Pretend you're wearing a strap on and we're going to have intercourse. Choose any position and simulate having sex with me but with me playing the woman.

Using the following words for inspiration, what new oral pleasuring ideas come to mind? SECONDS TREE THIGH SHIVERS BLINDFOLD THROBBING

 Have you ever secretly watched someone masturbate?

 What is the kinkiest type of foreplay activity that you have ever performed?

 On average, how long do you feel foreplay should last?

 What kind of erotic story or fantasy can you think of that is set in a jungle paradise?

 What classic literature most inspires your erotic fantasies?

Male Reads Question

 Have you ever given yourself a G-Spot orgasm? What technique did you use?

 What are the differences in the quality or intensity of your orgasm when having intercourse versus oral sex?

 What kinds of erotic roleplaying scenarios can you imagine the two of us doing together?

 What tips would you give to a young person wanting to have sex for the first time?

 What are your favorite online sex sites, and what do you like about them?

 If we were to play out a bondage fantasy scenario, how would you feel about roleplaying a captured spy being interrogated?

Female Reads Dare

 Demonstrate your favorite oral sex technique using any available fruit or vegetable.

 Place hot and steamy kisses all along my jaw from ear to ear.

 Use broad tongue strokes to lick slowly up and down my pussy. Use the underside of your tongue on my clitoris.

 Apply a nipple clamp (or smooth clothes peg) to one of my nipples. (not for too long)

 Lightly squeeze and tug my vaginal lips. Massage them delicately with moist fingertips.

 Describe how you would like me to stimulate your nipples. Then allow me to do as requested for 60 seconds. Clothing can be moved or removed to gain access if you desire.

Male Reads Dare

 Get a hand mirror and go somewhere private where I can still hear you. Examine and describe your pussy to me out loud.

 Suppose we were going to explore a gender swap roleplay scenario. Describe in detail how you would want either or both of us to prepare to make it as believable as possible.

 Describe in detail a design for an ultimate new sex toy or a creative new way to use one you already have. Include how we would play with it together.

 With me lying on my back, straddle me (no penetration). Rub my penis with your pussy while playing with your nipples and clitoris.

 Describe in detail what it feels like to experience a G-Spot orgasm.

 Describe what oral sex tastes like.

Female Reads Question

 Either alone or with a partner, have you ever used, or would you like to try using anal probes?

 Either alone or with a partner, have you ever used, or would you like to try using anal beads?

 If you were going to get a sex doll to play with, what features would it have?

 While shopping in a sex toy store, have you ever put a finger in a fake pussy to see what it feels like?

 If we were roleplaying a scenario involving me as an opposite-sex character, what name would you give me?

 Have you ever discovered anyone smelling your underwear or other used clothing for erotic reasons?

Male Reads Question

 Think of the characters and scenarios in your favorite television shows. Which ones would you most like to roleplay?

 How would you feel about roleplaying a "deflowering" scenario during that time of month?

 If you had the chance to watch a couple have sex, what would you want to see them doing?

 What was your experience like when you first performed oral sex?

 While performing a blow job, have you ever enhanced the sensation by sucking on black ball candies?

 What is your best foreplay tip if you were giving advice to a sexually inexperienced lesbian?

Use a piece of fur, silk or satin to smoothly caress any/all exposed parts of my body.

 Use an ice cube and your lips/tongue to cool then heat both my nipples. Then, do the same to stimulate my pussy and clitoris with hot and cold sensations.

 Describe in explicit detail what you would want me to do if you were tied up naked and spread-eagled on your back.

 Lightly drag your nails or fingertips all around my belly and along the crease above my hips to see if you can find a tickle zone.

 Describe in detail a fantasy scenario that involves you and me having sex with an element of BDSM.

 Make up a dirty joke using the following words: MASSAGE REAR ORALLY BUBBLE DESERT CANDLES

Male Reads Dare

 Caress and lightly stroke any/all exposed parts of my body.

 Smear a colorful, edible substance on your lips, then stroke my penis until it's erect enough to go down on. Attempt to deep throat as far as you can and leave your mark. (optionally use lipstick)

 Use a vibrator to stimulate my toes and soles of my feet.

 Describe in detail a new kinky activity that you "might" like to try (with or without me).

 Remove all clothing on our upper bodies. Apply massage oil to our chests and bellies. Then we'll slither and slide against each other while slow dancing to one song.

 Massage and fondle any part of my body still covered in clothing - do not touch any skin.

What kind of erotic story or fantasy can you think of that involves a twisted sex genie?

 When and where do you prefer to masturbate?

 What historical period, location or event most inspires your erotic thoughts?

 What color and type of lighting in the bedroom do you think is the sexiest?

 If we were to roleplay as strangers looking for anonymous sex, how many different scenarios can you think of?

 Have you ever experimented with cross-dressing, and if so, what kinds of clothing did you try on?

Male Reads Question

 What was the farthest you have ever squirted during a G-spot orgasm? How far do you think you could get if we tried right now?

 Do you ever masturbate without using a sex toy?

 What color and style of high heels do you think are the sexiest on a guy dressing up as a woman?

 What song do you feel has the best sexual euphemism?

 If you were going to create a sex-themed website, what domain name would you want, and what kind of content would you have on it?

 If you were to write me a sex coupon to be redeemed sometime later this week, what would it involve?

Put on an old shirt and let me passionately rip it off you.

 Expose and lightly lick my lower back and side. Lightly bite and nibble my buttocks.

 Kiss and lick any exposed erogenous zone you desire on my body.

 Get a blowup exercise ball or a big stack of pillows, then sit on or straddle it. Pretend there is a dildo attached. Bounce and grind on it with simulated sexual pleasure.

 Make up a short sexy blurb for an erotic movie pitch using the following words: THROES BRANDY VIGOROUS PIPE BEGUILE STIRRUPSEXSWING

 Reveal in explicit detail a fantasy with a "forced sex" element. Make up one if required.

Male Reads Dare

 I'll smear a colorful, edible substance on my lips. Allow me to open my mouth wide around one of your nipples and try to suck in as much of your tit as possible to mark a large ring. (optionally use lipstick)

 Imagine we are roleplaying a gender swap scenario. Pretend you're wearing a strap on and we're going to have intercourse in any woman on top position. Simulate having sex with me but with me playing the woman doing the thrusting.

 Allow me to apply nipple clamps (or smooth clothes pegs) to your nipples. (not for too long)

 See if you can put a condom on me using only your mouth. Use a flavored or novelty condom without spermicide.

 Describe in detail a fantasy scenario that involves you and me having sex with an element of risk or dangerous excitement.

 Drip melted wax on my chest or buttocks. (drip from far enough away to cool a bit and ensure it's not too hot to burn)

Female Reads Question

Whet Your Appetite With Wicked Words

 Imagine we mind swap with our partner every other time we have sex. We experience sex with their body, then switch back after our orgasms and a nap. How would this affect your desire to try new foreplay ideas?

 What is the most imaginative foreplay technique you have ever experienced or heard of?

 Using the following words for inspiration, what sex tips come to mind? RIPPEDBLOUSE TINGLY JOIN HORN THIGHSTRAPDILDO SNACK

 How do you feel about wearing high heels and stockings in bed while having sex?

 Have you ever masturbated using a piece of hollowed out fruit or vegetable like watermelon or squash?

 What is your favorite type of setting for self-pleasuring?

Male Reads Question

 Do you know what the term "Bend Over Boyfriend" means? Would you like to try it or learn more about it?

 Have you ever gone out in public with a butt plug inserted under your clothes?

 In what creative ways can you imagine pleasuring each other using a string of pearls?

 If you had the chance to watch a couple have sex, would you want to, and if so, who would you like to watch?

 Using the following words for inspiration, what is the trickiest sex related Yes/No questions you can think of? AROUSING GLOVE RELAX ECSTASY HEAVEN HAIR

 What tips do you think you could learn from lesbians to improve your lovemaking or relationship skills?

Female Reads Dare

 Tell a sexy story (real or made up) with explicit details that involves: A Short Stubby Dildo.

 Make up a dirty joke using the following words: CUSHION MOANING DONG BRUTAL BEAST THIGHSTRAPON

 Tell me what part of your body you want me to lick and suck on, then let me do it for 60 seconds.

 Hold a piece of frozen fruit (strawberry, mango, pineapple) in your mouth while you kiss me.

 Make up explicit details for a roleplay scenario based on: You polish an old bottle, and a sexy genie appears. Every wish or desire can be yours. But sexual energy fuels the genie's magic powers. If you want something, you'll have to work for it.

 Make up an erotic limerick (a verse of three long and two short lines rhyming scheme AABBA).

Male Reads Dare

 Go to the kitchen and get a dinner fork. Press it against one of my nipples so that parts are visible between the grooves, then flick your tongue over it.

 Creatively use a piece of furniture as a prop to make an erotic scene that involves you posing seductively.

 Make up a lost and found poster on a piece of paper for your favorite sex toy.

 Stimulate me with a sex toy. (Visual stimulation counts)

 On a single sheet of blank paper, draw the life-sized shape of a custom-designed butt plug for use in your sex play.

 Describe in detail a fantasy scenario that involves you and me enjoying anal sex play together.

What types of lingerie do you find most sexually exciting?

 In a fantasy or roleplaying scenario set in ancient times, would you rather be the witch or inquisitor?

 Do you prefer playing with sex toys for G-spot or clitoral orgasms?

 For someone of the opposite sex you find attractive, how would you describe the perfect eyes?

 Using the following words for inspiration, what new erotic adventure comes to mind? CLEAN FACESITTING FLOOD SAY ZIPPER CLIT

 How many different words, terms or names can you think of for the anus?

Male Reads Question

 What are the differences in the quality or intensity of your orgasm from manual versus oral stimulation?

 What is the wildest female fantasy you have ever read about, heard of or imagined?

 To give you the most pleasure or the best orgasm, what would be your top three tips to make cunnilingus amazing?

 What is the most daring outfit or lack of clothing you've worn or would like to wear out in public?

 How do you feel about anilingus?

 What is your best foreplay tip if you were giving advice to a sexually inexperienced man?

Describe in detail how you would include a strap-on with me in a new sex position or other playful activity. If I have one, entice me to get it on and have a bit of fun.

 Go in for an intimate kiss with me but freeze just before our lips touch each other. Stay as close as possible for 60 seconds, then finish the kiss.

 Use a feather or piece of silky material to tickle my face, lips, ears and neck.

 I will smear a colorful, edible substance on my lips. Allow me to stroke your penis until it's erect enough to go down on. Then, I'll deep throat you as far as I can to leave my mark. (optionally use lipstick)

 Tell a sexy story (real or made up) with explicit details that involves: A Blue Vibrator.

 Make up a short sexy blurb for an erotic movie pitch using the following words: MIST ROUGHSEX ANKLECUFFS MILKY FEET WAND

Male Reads Dare

 Get into a doggie style position with me but with no penetration. I will remain still while you wiggle and circle your pelvis against me.

 Play-wrestle with me and see if you can pin me down for a kiss.

 Find a dildo or other suitable phallic object. I'll hold it while you demonstrate a sensual "boob job". Use lube or vegetable oil if desired.

 For 60 seconds, use one of your hands and your mouth to separately stimulate two different parts of my body simultaneously.

 Make up a short sexy blurb for an erotic novel pitch using the following words: DOUBLE SEXERCISE NIPPLERING ERECTION RING PURRING

 Get me into a position to receive oral sex and simulate how you would perform it. Moan and hum with enthusiasm for added effect.

Female Reads Question

Frisky Foreplay Feels Fantastic

 Suppose we were both sentenced to house arrest together for 5 months with no other responsibilities. What kinds of things do you think we would order online to ensure our sex play never got boring?

 In a fantasy or roleplaying scenario set in ancient times, would you rather be the barbarian or missionary?

 What is your best tip or technique for performing great oral sex on a woman?

 What is the largest dildo you have ever used vaginally?

 How did you react the first time you saw someone of the opposite sex peeing?

 If we were to make a video of an erotic puppet show, what kind of naughty scenario would you want to perform, and what kind of props would you like to include in the show?

Male Reads Question

 Would you find it more thrilling to secretly watch me play with myself or be invited to watch?

 Imagine we mind swap with our partner every other time we have sex. We experience sex with their body, then switch back after our orgasms and a nap. How would this affect your desire to receive oral sex?

 Would you prefer balls attached to your dildos for realism, or would you choose some other type of grip?

 What is your best foreplay tip if you were giving advice to a sexually inexperienced gay guy?

 What parts of your body do you most enjoy getting massaged?

 Do you like something in your vagina while your clitoris is stimulated to orgasm either orally, manually or with a vibrator?

Pleasure yourself with a sex toy while I watch.

 Lying down so your head is hanging over an accessible edge (bed, table, sofa, etc.), orally pleasure my pussy.

 Using lube and two fingers, massage my pussy. Penetrate my vagina with smooth, gliding strokes.

 Make up explicit details for a roleplay scenario based on: A woman is haunted by dreams of extreme lust – lewd and nasty acts of depravity. An exorcist is called in to help free these sexual demons from her mind and body.

 Kiss and lick the soft, sensitive skin behind my knees.

 Make up explicit details for a roleplay scenario based on: You're a casting agent, and she's a model looking to get into the business.

Male Reads Dare

 Make up explicit details for a roleplay scenario based on: She's an innocent prairie farm girl caught masturbating in a field by a roving cowboy.

 Make up a sexy incantation or spell using the following words: REDWINE SWALLOWED ROD GUIDE RAUNCHY AFTERCARE

 Orally pleasure the head of my penis with a mint, some liquor or a dab of toothpaste in your mouth. Warming flavored lube is good too.

 Pretend you are having sex with a ghost partner that only you can see and feel.

 Dab some ice cream or smear a popsicle on my nipples and lick them clean.

 Make up explicit details for a roleplay scenario based on: You're the kidnapper of a very attractive hostage with a pristine reputation. To ensure your demands are met, a blackmail video is made.

Female Reads Question

 If you were alone with someone of the same sex who was attractive to you and receptive, how would you feel about performing oral sex?

 Using the following words for inspiration, what Either-Or type sex question would you most like to ask your closest friend? BAMBOOCANE FLICKS OPENING STIFF FLASHLIGHT NIBBLER

 What would you do to me if you had me tied up and blindfolded?

 How are your orgasms different when using a sex toy versus when you don't?

 Using the following words for inspiration, what is the trickiest sex related Either-Or questions you can think of? STAFF SPHINCTER AROUSED PADDEDCUFFS CARNAL BRUSH

 Would you ever consider timing yourself to determine the fastest time it takes to get an erection from a flaccid state? What technique would you use or want to be used?

Male Reads Question

 if you were to use a sex toy for men to enhance your foreplay with new stimulating sensations, what kind would it be, and how would you want to use it?

 What do you like and dislike about having sex in the missionary position?

 What tips or techniques do you think guys need to know about pleasuring a woman with their fingers?

 Using the following words for inspiration, what title would you give to an erotic movie that I star in? PULSE FRICTION ALLURING PREACHER CONNECT DARKCHOCOLATE

 What words or phrases do you use or associate with having an orgasm?

 Have you ever purchased a shower head for its potential as a masturbation aid?

Female Reads Dare

 I will play as your Love Slave. Sternly command me to perform and service one of your desires.

 Find, then use an item with an interesting texture to stimulate and sensitize an exposed region of my body. (soft, cold, rough, squishy, etc.)

 In a missionary or doggie style position, penetrate my vagina once as slowly and deeply as you can – I am not allowed to move.

 Use a dildo and some lube to demonstrate how you would like me to give you a hand job.

 Make up explicit details for a roleplay scenario based on: He's a Sultan reclining on a mound of pillows and decides he wants some erotic entertainment. He claps three times to signal his harem or slave girl to enter.

 While maintaining eye contact, kiss me from toes to lips and back down again.

Male Reads Dare

 Kneeling while I stand, kiss and lick my belly, hips and thighs. Knead and massage my buttocks.

 Apply nipple clamps (or smooth clothes pegs) to your nipples. (not for too long)

 Using the following words for inspiration, describe a scenario that involves lots of lube and awesome sexplay: THROES IMAGINE FINGERS FRENZIED CLITORALSUCKER BUTTPLUG

 Find a short piece of erotica in a book, magazine or on the internet and read it out loud as seductively as you can.

 Lightly squeeze and tug my scrotum (ball sack). Gently play with my testicles.

 Use a piece of soft, juicy, sticky fruit. Rub it on my penis, then lick it clean.

What's the strangest thing you've done or thought about to avoid premature ejaculation?

 If you were to try out erotic roleplay as space aliens, what non-human color and texture of skin would you find attractive?

 What creatively sensual activities can you imagine doing to each other with chocolate?

 Have you ever listened to a sexual hypnosis or self-improvement CD?

 What is your favorite position for having wild, intense sex?

 What kinds of pornography have you seen, and which types do you like best?

Male Reads Question

 If creating a piece of erotic art together using our naked bodies, which style of artwork would you prefer? A: Apply paint to our bodies and make an impression on canvas, or B: Create a plaster cast of parts of our bodies to make a statue

 If you worked in the sex industry, would you rather be A: a stripper or B: a porn star?

 If orgasms created flashes of color or images in your mind, what colors or images would you see?

 What was your experience like when you first received oral sex?

 Have you ever slow danced naked before making love?

 What kinds of sex play do you think we could perform if we had to keep our butts cheek to cheek?

Female Reads Dare

 Make up explicit details for a roleplay scenario based on: A young witch discovers a dark spell that only a virgin can perform. Lusting for power, she conjures up a demon lover (devil, vampire, werewolf) to ravish her and fulfill the ritual.

 Attempt to give me a G-Spot orgasm and make me squirt using just your fingers.

 Do an internet search for Knotted Dildo and browse a few of the results listed.

 Look into my eyes as you suck one of my fingers and manually pleasure my pussy.

 Light a candle and allow me to drip some warm, melted wax somewhere on your body. (drip from far enough away to cool a bit and ensure it's not too hot to burn)

 Make up an Invitation Card to a romantic or risqué liaison for the two of us using the following words: INVENT DIRTIEST SLIME BACK SHAGGED FIREPLACE

Male Reads Dare

 Tell a sexy story (real or made up) with explicit details that involves: A Sex Swing.

 Tell a sexy story (real or made up) with explicit details that involves: A Leather Spanker.

 Make up explicit details for a roleplay scenario based on: You're a doctor with a patient who requires a completely thorough physical examination.

 Redress into a new piece of visually and sensually erotic lingerie that you know will arouse me.

 Suck one of my fingers while manually pleasuring my penis. (do not remove any clothing)

 Tickle my testicles, inner thighs and perineum with your tongue. Flutter your tongue like a flickering flame.

Female Reads Question

Get Dirty And Nasty!

 What's the least expensive sex toy you own?

 Have you ever used hot sauce to spice up your sex life?

 What is the strangest or most creative thing you've used to stimulate yourself or a lover?

 If you had to give verbal instructions to someone about to make love for the first time, what would you say to help them perform satisfying intercourse?

 In a fantasy or roleplaying scenario set in ancient times, would you rather be the high priest or worshiper?

 Do you know what the sexual term ATM stands for?

Male Reads Question

 Have you ever used a special prostate massager on a male partner?

 If you were to design the ultimate sex toy for either women, men or couples, how would it look, and what features would it have?

 What kind of erotic story or fantasy can you think of that involves a sexy "monster"?

 What foods or smells get you turned on or thinking about having sex?

 What is the most romantic trip or vacation you've dreamed about, and what sexy activities would you like to do there?

 Have you ever had intercourse with a butt plug inserted?

 Bend over and allow me to insert a lubricated butt plug – remove it only when we're finished playing.

 Apply lube to my nipples and stimulate them with the head of your cock.

 Tell a sexy story (real or made up) with explicit details that involves: A Red Vibrator.

 Go to a different location in the house with me and enjoy 30 seconds of intercourse in a creative position of your choice.

 Put on a sexy song with a strong rhythm and perform a sexy belly dance as best you can.

 Using the most realistic dildo or phallic object available, move it across the room with me using only our mouths.

Male Reads Dare

 Allow me to clip/trim your pubic hair.

 Make up explicit details for a roleplay scenario based on: You're a prison guard and she's a new prisoner who needs to be shown how things work.

 Make up explicit details for a roleplay scenario based on: She's a casting agent, and he's a model looking to get into the business.

 Make up explicit details for a roleplay scenario based on: You are a highly trained spy seducing a scientist at a top-secret lab. You must gain access to their computers.

 Make up a short sexy blurb for an erotic novel pitch using the following words: REACH FLOWING ESCORT CANDLES TOYING GENITALS

 Using the following words for inspiration, describe a scenario that involves amazing oral delights: HANDLE PRIVATE YESMISTRESS ZIPPER LICKED GYRATE

Female Reads Question

 In porn, what kind of money shot do you find is the most erotic? Do you prefer to see the guy pull out to ejaculate or see a "cream pie"?

 In a "forced sex" fantasy or roleplaying scenario, would you rather be A: the kidnapper or B: the hostage?

 Do you prefer playing with hard or soft vibrators?

 What one part of my body do you find most Kissable?

 How do you feel about mixing in anilingus while performing cunnilingus?

 How would you feel about searching the internet together with me for erotic art to purchase or add to a private digital image collection?

Male Reads Question

 Have you ever used body paints or markers for fun sex play?

 How do you feel about "make up" sex compared to "normal" lovemaking?

 At what age did you first see an adult movie with sex? How explicit was it, and what feelings do you remember having?

 In a "forced sex" fantasy or roleplaying scenario, would you rather be A: the pirate or B: the captive?

 How many different sex positions can you think of in 30 seconds?

 How do you think couples can arrange their day so they have lots of time to enjoy more foreplay together?

Female Reads Dare

Carnal Knowledge Confessions

 With a flickering tongue, lick from one of my nipples, down past my belly button (as far as you dare), then up again to the other nipple. If not yet accessible, adjust clothing if required to get as close as possible without revealing them.

 Slide your hand up the back of my neck, spread your fingers slightly in the hair and grab a handful. Assert a sense of dominance by tugging or pulling my hair with a firm grip. (no hair yanking)

 Describe a possible self pleasuring activity using the following words: LIGHT EQUIPMENT PENETRATION GRINDS REAR BONDAGECOLLAR

 Creatively stimulate me with a vibrator. (Visual stimulation counts)

 Get a hand mirror and go somewhere private where I can still hear you. Examine and describe your butt hole to me out loud.

 In a missionary position, lift my legs high and penetrate me deeply. Lick and suck on my toes to make me wiggle on your cock.

Male Reads Dare

 Make up explicit details for a roleplay scenario based on: He's a casting agent, and she's a model looking to get into the business.

 Give me a rim job (oral-anal pleasuring). Use a dental dam (plastic wrap) and flavored lube.

 Select, lube up, and self-insert a butt plug or anal dildo of your choice.

 Give me a foot job – apply lube and use your toes and the soles of your feet to stimulate my penis.

 Apply flavored lube to my penis and rub your nipples with it. Finish by licking the lube off my dick, and I'll lick it off your nipples.

 Smear a spicy hot sauce around your lips and then kiss me passionately. After your kiss, let me lick and suck it off your lips.

Female Reads Question

 Where would you most like to go for a vacation if the sole purpose was to have the best sex of your life?

 How do you feel about experimenting with bondage?

 What forms of public affection make you feel more embarrassed than turned on?

 What same-sex scenarios or fantasies, if any, would you consider roleplaying?

 Of all the types of sex play activities you can think of or have experienced, what is the most naughty or forbidden?

 Do you find it more erotic and arousing watching a woman or man masturbate?

Male Reads Question

 What length and thickness do you feel would make the best-sized penis for oral sex?

 What color and type of lighting in the bedroom do you think is the most Erotic?

 Using the following words for inspiration, what Either-Or type sex question would you most like to ask your closest friend? PINKNIPPLES LICKED MADEOUT MONSTER LAVISH TASSEL

 Would you rather redo or relive the first romantic kiss you ever had?

 In what situations would you forego foreplay and just have sex?

 Have you ever masturbated using the vibrations of a running washing machine or dryer?

Female Reads Dare

 For the next 60 seconds, stimulate your nipples using your fingers.

 Make up explicit details for a roleplay scenario based on: She's a teacher in a private college with one student who desperately needs one on one tutoring after hours. She knows just how to motivate him.

 Using the following words for inspiration, describe a scenario that involves amazing oral delights: JAM YANK BRUTAL ASSHOLE DUNGEONMASTER BIKINIWAX

 Insert one finger in my vagina (moisten if necessary) and gently massage left, right, up, down and all around – no thrusting.

 Stand behind me in front of a mirror and watch me as you stroke and fondle my body intimately.

 Using only your hands, demonstrate a favorite foreplay or sex play technique.

Male Reads Dare

 Make up explicit details for a roleplay scenario based on: He's an angel seduced by a demon that can take on any form.

 Perform a slow romantic dance with a pretend or ghost partner.

 Rub and massage my crotch (through my clothing if I'm still wearing any).

 Put on some "old" underwear so I can rip them off of you passionately and ravish you orally. (pre-cut the elastic band if necessary)

 Suck on the shaft of my penis. Slide your lips up and down the sides of my erection as you lick and flick with your tongue.

 Lightly tug small amounts of pubic hair all around my genital region.

Have you ever looked into a lover's eyes as you or they were having an orgasm?

 In what way would you most like to add the "thrill of getting caught" to your sex play to make it even more exciting?

 How do you feel about facials or ejaculation on other body parts?

 Have you ever used a special prostate massager?

 What kind of erotic story or fantasy can you think of that is set on a tropical island?

 What is your favorite erotic video, and what aspects of it do you like the most?

Male Reads Question

 How do you feel about using a strap-on dildo for "pegging" (anal sex with a guy)?

 What erotic fantasies, sexy stories or roleplaying scenarios can you think of that would fit the title Bound to Please?

 Suppose you were to play out a fairy tale fantasy scenario. What kinds of erotic roleplaying scenarios can you think of based on any characters, scenes or settings found in Arabian Nights?

 If you could customize the design of your favorite sex toy, what colors would you use?

 If you were "forced" into the sex industry, would your erotic talents enable you to make more money as a dominatrix, porn star, sex cam operator, prostitute or escort?

 Using the following words for inspiration, what title would you give to an erotic movie that I star in? DEFLOWER ANALSPOONING SOAKING MELON GUIDE BODY

Female Reads Dare

Erotic Expressions
Excite Everyone

 Get a large teddy bear or pillow. Pretend it's me you're making out with. (simulate enthusiastic loving without getting it dirty though)

 Search the internet and find a short porn video involving gay sex and watch it with me.

 Go to the kitchen and get a dinner fork. Use it to sensually stimulate me by dragging it lightly across an exposed region of my body.

 Using a flavored lube, massage a few of my toes, then lick and suck on them.

 Allow me to give you a prostate massage.

 Kiss and lick my wrist, inner arm and elbow.

Male Reads Dare

 Suppose you were about to list me on a sex-for-money site. Quickly write/draw a short ad to sell my unique services.

 Suppose you changed into a male for an hour and could have sex with any female. Tell me who it would be with and what you would do. Describe the sex in detail.

 With me standing, kneel behind, then nibble and bite my buttocks while playing with my penis and testicles.

 Put on a piece of clothing or accessory (leather, stockings, boots, high heels, etc.) that you know will drive me crazy with desire.

 Reveal in explicit detail a fantasy with a "forced sex" element that involves me. Make up one if required.

 Make up explicit details for a roleplay scenario based on: He's a doctor with a patient who requires a completely thorough physical examination.

Female Reads Question

Joys Of Juicy Sex

 Suppose you were my secret sex Santa. What is the strangest sex toy present you think would shock me?

 Would you rather roleplay as a sexy yet innocent angel or a hot and naughty devil? Describe how you would look or behave.

 How would you react if I made you a video of myself masturbating?

 If you were given a chance to see all the sexual thoughts, dreams and fantasies of just one person other than me, whose mind would you want to read, and what do you think you would see?

 How do you feel about experimenting with foot fetish play?

 What kind of erotic cartoon or animated fantasy can you imagine where we are the main characters? What characters would we each play?

Male Reads Question

 If we were to get frisky together as "furries", what style and color of furry costumes would you choose for us to fool around in?

 How much and what kinds of foreplay do you feel is best before anal intercourse?

 Consider the term "pushing rope". What other names or phrases have you heard for this type of situation?

 Suppose you were to play out a fairy tale fantasy scenario. What kinds of erotic roleplaying scenarios can you think of based on any characters, scenes or settings found in your favorite story?

 Using the following words for inspiration, what new erotic adventure comes to mind? COOL STOP RAIN SLONG BOOK SHAVE

 What aspect of your sex life would you be willing to give up or receive in exchange for $10,000?

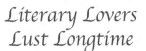
 Do an internet search for Knotted Dildo, browse a few of the results listed, and purchase one.

 Orally pleasure my entire pussy. Use creative licking and sucking techniques.

 Entice me to put on some "old" underwear. Then, rip them off of me passionately and ravish me orally. (pre-cut the elastic band if necessary)

 Warm or cool a glass or acrylic dildo and pleasure me with it.

 Imagine we are roleplaying a gender swap scenario. Pretend I am wearing a strap on and we're going to have intercourse in any woman on top position. Simulate having sex with me but with you playing the woman doing the thrusting.

 Look through an explicit pictorial magazine or book with me. Discuss what you consider erotic and arousing.

Male Reads Dare

 Try to take my underwear off using just your mouth.

 Kiss and lightly lick my hand, palm and fingers. Choose my non-dominant hand.

 Sensuously demonstrate fellatio using a sex toy or edible object. Close your eyes and pretend it's my penis.

 Allow me to use an implement of my choice to erotically spank your bare ass until it radiates a sensual heat. I'll caress and stroke it between smacks.

 Describe in explicit detail what you would do to me if I were tied up naked and spread-eagled on my back.

 Watch one scene of an XXX DVD with me. You choose the DVD.

What is the fastest time you can remember that you made someone orgasm with oral sex?

 Do you enjoy being watched while performing oral sex?

 For someone of the opposite sex you find attractive, how would you describe the perfect chest?

 What kind of erotic story or fantasy can you think of that is set in a mystical place?

 While working out together at a gym, you discover we're all alone and you're feeling naughty. Where would you rather have sex? A: On any convenient exercise equipment or B: In the shower, sauna or tanning booth

 How kinky or sexually adventurous do you feel you are?

Male Reads Question

 How would you spice up the rules for any two-player card game to make it a sex game for couples to play together?

 How much foreplay do you desire on average before the main event? What's your signal that you're ready for more?

 What is the largest dildo you have ever used anally?

 What is the fastest time you can remember that you orgasmed when having sex?

 Suppose you were to write a letter to a sex magazine involving the two of us doing something wild. What would it be about if it had to be realistic but not necessarily true?

 On what days and times of day do you most feel like making love?

Female Reads Dare

  Pondering Passionate Possibilities

 Use an implement of your choice to erotically spank my bare ass until it radiates a sensual heat. Caress and stroke it between smacks.

 Use a digital camera with a zoom lens to take very close-up and intimate shots of my erogenous zones. Select one to print and frame and delete the rest.

 Make up explicit details for a roleplay scenario based on: He's a high ranking officer in uniform and she's a public official looking to develop a special liaison.

 Smear a colorful, edible substance on your lips. Open your mouth wide around one of my nipples and try to suck in as much of my tit as possible to mark a large ring. (optionally use lipstick)

 With me laying on the floor, get on top and simulate having sex together but with me performing all the thrusting or grinding motions.

 Quickly go somewhere private with a cell phone and take a very close up picture of a part of you. Zoom and crop it to show only a single sexy feature before revealing it to me.

Male Reads Dare

 Expose, then pinch, tweak and twiddle your nipples. Use lube if desired. Then, have me suck and bite them gently.

 Sensually trace your tongue around an exposed part of my body. Then softly blow cool air on the area to dry the moist trail.

 Make up a short sexy phrase or expression for an Orgy Invitation Card using the following words: BERRIES GOBBLE PEGME WINDOW LAP ENTIRE

 I'll pulse my PC muscles as tightly and quickly as I can for a minute while you cup my crotch in one hand. I'll try to make you feel my dick twitch.

 Allow me to use an implement of your choice to erotically spank your bare ass until it radiates a sensual heat. I'll caress and stroke it between smacks.

 Using a firm, pointed tongue, lick my perineum and base of my scrotum using circles, swirls and zigzag strokes.

Female Reads Question

 How are your orgasms different when masturbating compared to when you have sex?

 Imagine we mind swap with our partner every other time we have sex. We experience sex with their body, then switch back after our orgasms and a nap. How would this affect your desire to try new sex positions?

 How many different words, terms or names can you think of for anal sex?

 If there was a lull in your sex life, how would you re-ignite your sexual desire?

 How do you think male and female orgasms compare?

 What style and color of leather or latex outfit would you like to see either of us wear?

Male Reads Question

 How many different words, terms or names can you think of for female privates?

 What is the weirdest or most surprising sexual activity a lover has tried with you?

 Suppose we would have another person or couple join us for a sexual adventure together. Who would you want to get together with, and how would you imagine us doing it?

 What is the most intriguing term you've heard for a kinky sex or fetish activity?

 Have you ever felt an instant sexual connection with someone off-limits?

 How kinky or sexually adventurous do you feel we could be together?

Describe in detail a new and exciting place to make love. Include activities you would like to experience so we can dream them together.

 Make up explicit details for a roleplay scenario based on: He's a sex researcher hunting for proof that the mythical G-Spot exists. She's the willing volunteer helping him in the search to unlock its orgasmic potential.

 Select something sexy for me to wear right now.

 Delicately massage my clitoris and vaginal lips with a lubricant. Lovingly look into my eyes and discover how I respond to your touch.

 Give me a brief but relaxing massage the way you know I like it.

 Tell a sexy story (real or made up) with explicit details that involves: Anal Beads.

Male Reads Dare

 Demonstrate how you would like a hand job performed by simulating the action yourself.

 Get into a "69" position with you on top of me so we can pleasure each other orally.

 Circle my scrotum just above my testicles with your thumb and index finger. Pull down on my sack until taut and lick my testicles.

 Make up a short sexy blurb for an erotic novel pitch using the following words: SILKY CLOTHESPIN TITTIES ROLEPLAYING ROSEBUDDEFLOWERING RECOIL

 While I sit, perform an erotic dance for me to one song of your choice. Seductively entice me to caress and fondle your assets.

 Find and creatively use a non-sexual object to pleasure me.

 What style of electronic communication would you prefer if you were going to experiment with cybersex?

 What makes for a great kiss?

 How would you spice up the rules for Eight Ball Pool to make it a sex game for couples to play together?

 If you were alone with someone of the same sex who was attractive to you and receptive, how would you feel about performing a hand job?

 If you were to play out a "deflowering" fantasy scenario, how would you feel about roleplaying one with a ritual virgin sacrifice involving ... (make up the rest of the question)?

 Given the title Passionate Politician, what roleplay scenario, fantasy or erotic story can you imagine for it?

Male Reads Question

 What erotic fantasies, sexy stories or roleplaying scenarios can you think of that would fit the title It's Just Business?

 On a hot summer day, have you ever tried sex in the rain? Would you like to try it?

 How long does it usually take you to stimulate yourself to orgasm?

 If we were to experiment with bondage or SM play, what safe word would you like to stop our sex play if it gets too intense?

 What creative sex positions can you imagine performing using any piece of furniture available right now?

 Using the following words for inspiration, what sex-related superpower would you most like to have and why? PUSSYPUNISHING ORIFICE MOVIE TREMBLE VIGOROUSLY TENSION

Female Reads Dare

 Do an internet search for Clit Suction Toys and browse a few of the results listed.

 Using a wall or door, pretend you have just entered a "glory hole" and are in the process of getting "serviced".

 Describe a possible erotic fantasy using the following words: HARD INVENT LIQUOR CRACK BIKINIWAX CLITSUCKER

 Using lube, insert your two middle fingers into my vagina with palm on my clitoris. Flutter your fingers up and down quickly to trigger a G-Spot orgasm.

 Pleasure yourself with an anal dildo or butt plug while I watch.

 After I put on an old shirt, passionately rip it off as if you're hot with lust.

Male Reads Dare

 Apply some lube between your butt cheeks. With me standing up against a wall, rub and stroke my penis with your hot buns.

 Stimulate me with a butt plug or anal dildo. (Visual stimulation counts)

 Describe a Christmas themed roleplay scenario or fantasy that you would enjoy.

 Tell a sexy story (real or made up) with explicit details that involves: Velcro Bondage Cuffs.

 With broad, luscious tongue strokes, lick all around the shaft of my penis. Put the head in your mouth and suck it briefly.

 Make up explicit details for a roleplay scenario based on: Two virgins are eager to consummate their love on their wedding night.

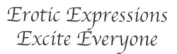

Female Reads Question

Erotic Expressions
Excite Everyone

 When using a dildo for sex play, either solo or with a partner, have you ever attached it to something for hands-free play?

 In a sci-fi fantasy or roleplaying scenario, would you rather be A: Star Trek or B: Star Wars characters?

 When was the last time you got dirty in the shower, and what were you doing?

 Do you enjoy or think you would enjoy the feel of hard cold glass or steel butt plugs?

 Given the title Paid For Pleasure, what roleplay scenario, fantasy or erotic story can you imagine for it?

 How do you think people can recreate the exciting sexual curiosity of their first make out sessions?

Male Reads Question

 Have you ever included choking in your sex play?

 How many different sex positions do you think we can get into in one minute?

 Using the following words for inspiration, what sex-magic spell would you most like to use on me? SILKSCARF MADEOUT ROCK PALM SPIT OUTSTRETCHED

 What erotic fantasies, sexy stories or roleplaying scenarios can you think of that would fit the title Caught by Surprise?

 Using the following words for inspiration, what title would you give to an erotic movie that you star in? LACEBRA SHOT CHASTITYBELT OBSCENE MANHOOD POKE

 Have you ever named a sex toy after one of your lovers, a famous person or someone you lusted after? If so, which toy and what name did you give it? If not, pick a toy you own and give it a sexy name.

Insert a dildo of my choice into my pussy while licking my clitoris. Move the dildo in slow, smooth strokes.

 Creatively stimulate me any way you desire.

 While I use my fingers to expose my clitoris for you, use only the soft underside of your tongue to delicately caress and stroke it.

 Go into the bathroom and dab a scent somewhere on your body, then come back and let me sniff you until I find where you put it.

 Make up explicit details for a roleplay scenario based on: He's a virgin wanting to explore sex with a more experienced woman. He wants her to teach him how to pleasure his future wife.

 Make up explicit details for a roleplay scenario based on: A patient is getting a free medical procedure in exchange for being observed by a group of interns.

Male Reads Dare

 Your choice of a Nasty, Kinky or Taboo foreplay activity – surprise me with your wild side.

 Have 30 seconds of intercourse with me in a doggie style position.

 Tell a sexy story (real or made up) with explicit details that involves: An Appearance Changing Wig.

 Make up explicit details for a roleplay scenario based on: He's been hunting the Queen of Darkness in her lair. But, night has fallen, and he has stumbled into her trap. Now, under her control, he's bound and displayed for her sadistic pleasure.

 Give me a prostate massage.

 Roleplaying as a Love Slave, submissively request my desire, then perform the sexual favor for your master.

Female Makes Up:

  Double Dirty Dares

 A "Sensual Pleasuring" dare involving: TONGUEINTWAT CERAMICCOCKS BREAST CLEAN OBEY ORALBLISS

 A "Foreplay Fun With Food" dare inspired by: CIRCLE BEAD HYPNOGASM HIP HORNY HAIRYPUSSY

 An "Impersonate <person> Having Sex" dare inspired by: EVERY PLANT SLEEK GSPOTGASP PRIVATE SILKSTOCKINGS

 A "Describe A Kinky Sex Dungeon Scene" dare inspired by: ALLURING FUCKSTANDING PICTURE JEWEL DERRIERE RIDE

 A "Pretend Bondage Ravishment" dare inspired by: SCREW SLIME BUN BARENAKED MUSK BUTTSLAPPER

 An "Impersonate <person> Having Sex" dare inspired by: FUCKEDSILLY PICTURE THIGHS RINSE PENETRATING MAD

Male Makes Up:

 An "As My Submissive, Beg Me" dare using: OVERFLOW BUSHWHACKING CHOCOLATE PASSIONATELY STRADDLE CHEEK

 A "Mime An Extra Nasty Activity" inspired by: TURN EYECONTACT NIPPLEORGASM HEART REVERSE GOO

 A "Historic Themed Erotic" dare using: CANDLE CONNECT LESBIANS CHASINGTAIL ANUS LIQUID

 A "Pretend Bondage Ravishment" dare inspired by: POLE TRUST TASSEL WIDE NUTSACKNIBBLER GSPOT

 A "Detail Sex In Wild Location" dare inspired by: HEAT TORNBLOUSE NERVE PENETRATION SCREWMENOW FRENCHKISSING

 A "Pretend Magical Gender Swap" dare inspired by: ICY MAKELOVE BACKDOOR APPLY NEEDLEPLAY SOUND

Female Makes Up:

 A "Live Sex Demonstration" dare featuring: FLING BELLYBUTTON JUICY PRISONWIFE FLOGGER TIGHTSPOT

 A "Create Special Holiday Card For Me" dare using: SPHINCTER PUDDLEJUMPING PULL LINGERIE UPTHEASS EAGER

 A "Sensual Pleasuring" dare involving: ENGORGED DOITANYWAY WORSHIP SCARF MALE EXPLOSIVEORGASM

 A "Crossdressing" dare inspired by: CHOCOLATE REVEALED HARDASS THRUST CUNTSICLE BROWNNIPPLES

 A "Detail Sex In Wild Location" dare using: DRIP BENDOVERBITCH CLITONCLIT YUMMY BALLS MONEY

 A "Self-Pleasuring" dare involving: COLD HAIRYCUNT OIL DEEPTHROATING BUTTCHEEKS BLEND

Male Makes Up:

 An "Explicit Details For A Roleplay Scenario" dare inspired by: LUBRICATION WORKITGIRL BUM POP RAMITIN EROTICALLY

 A "Detail Nastiest Imaginable Masturbation Act Done By <person>" dare using: SPHINCTER EARLOBENIBBLE DARKCHOCOLATE POUNDMYASS LAUNCH PLAYFUL

 A "Dark Fantasy Roleplay" dare using: ANAL CUNTWEBS TRUST DUCTTAPE SHALLOW EATCREAMPIE

 A "Create Special Holiday Card For Me" dare using: CANDY TITTIEFUCKING BLOW PRISONWIFESWAP DONG PLIANT

 A "Sex For Money" dare using: NIBBLES TRHOBBINGCLIT SPUNK BUTTHOLEFUCKER CUFF BARENAKED

 A "Detail Sex In Wild Location" dare inspired by: DRAG CAMCORDER TONGUE SWELL HARDERFASTER SEXYBEAST

An "Explicit Details For A Roleplay Scenario" dare using: TORNBLOUSE ENGORGEDCLIT CUNTLICKER SCHLONG STRAIGHTPORN DESCRIBE

 A "Sex For Money" dare using: SEXTOYS FLICKERINGTONGUE PET PIGTAILREINS GLANS GLASSJUICER

 A "Draft A Ridiculous Sex Law" dare using: LACEPANTIES JERKMEOFF SQUASH THICKSHAFT HEEL SLUTTYCUNT

 An "As My Submissive, Beg Me" dare using: LIMPDICK PANT PEARLNECKLACE TESTICLE BLOWJOBQUEEN DARKCHOCOLATE

 An "Explicit Details For A Roleplay Scenario" dare inspired by: NIPPLES UPTHEASS TEASES BUTTHOLEFUCKER SEEPINGSLIT CLITCLIP

 A "Dark Fantasy Roleplay" dare using: ANALANCHOR SWEETCUNT CHOCOLATESAUCE BRUSH JIZZJUNKY WRIST

Male Makes Up:

 A "Crossdressing" dare using: CLITNIBBLER GRABASS TESTOSTERONE SWEETLIQUOR ACHE TEABAGGING

 A "Physically Pleasure Me" dare inspired by: SUGAR VULVA TWOCOCKS FIRE FISHTACO TITTYFUCK

 A "Sci-Fi Themed Erotic" dare using: LABIALOVING LESBIANPORN ANUS FUCKMYTITS SLITHER CUP

 A "Detail Sex In Wild Location" dare using: LACEPANTIES VAGINALANCHOR ONEEYEDEEL BUSH TRICKLE YESPLEASE

 A "Sensual Pleasuring" dare involving: COCK LYINGEYES HAT WRONGHOLE GRINDING ROCKHARD

 A "Sexy Word Challenge" dare using: FINGER CARAMEL THINK FORBIDDENHOLE FRESHMEAT TIGHTTWATS

Female Makes Up:

  Double Dirty Dares

 A "Sci-Fi Themed Erotic" dare using: QUIVERINGQUIM TOES FUDGEPACKER SQUIRT BUSHWHACKING DOMEBABY

 A "Historic Themed Erotic" dare using: FOOTJOB TONGUEINCHEEK TOECURLINGCLIMAX JUGS HUG NIBBLEMYCLIT

 A "Crossdressing" dare using: PRECUMDRIP GOLDENSPRINKLES SHAVE WANG LIPSTICKLESBIAN SUCKHERTOES

 A "Sex Education Lesson" dare featuring: SURPRISE HANDHELDDILDO NIPPLES PUSSYPOUNDING LICKMYSLIT FURRYTWAT

 An "Arouse Me Aurally" dare involving: TRIBADISM FINGERINGMYASS HUMBLING SWOLLENLIPS REAR CONTROL

 A "Do Something Nasty" dare using: THROBBINGCOCK SLURP JIZZONME NAIL TASTYTOES SEXYBEAST

Male Makes Up:

 A "Detail Sex In Wild Location" dare inspired by: TITTYFUCKING HANDSFREEFUCKING TEMPT SWALLOWMYLOAD SWALLOWMYJIZZ BEHIND

 A "Detail Nastiest Imaginable Sex Act Between ..." dare using: SITONMYCOCK GSPOTSPRAY BUN SOURCUNT LESBIANFANTASY FLAUNT

 A "Sexy Word Challenge" dare using: SHAGHAG SKANKYWHORE TUNNEL BUSHWHACKING GOODGIRL GRINDING

 An "Alternate Sexual Orientation" dare using: PUSSYSLAPPING FOREHEAD PLEASE SEEPINGSLIT NAUGHTYKNICKERS BALLSTRETCHER

 A "Sexy Word Challenge" dare using: JIZZJUNKY FUCKMYCUNT ANALFINGERING TRIPLEDICKED GUSH GSPOT

 An "Allow Me To Pleasure You" dare inspired by: DIRTYWHORE WIFESHARING SHAVEDCUNT SQUIRT SWEETPOONTANG ANUS

Double Dirty Dares

Female Makes Up:

 A "Pretend Bondage Ravishment" dare using: BLUEBALLS SKANKY DONKEYDILDO HARDON TITBONDAGE DYKE

 A "Dark Fantasy Roleplay" dare inspired by: KNOB SMELLMYCUNT FURRYFEAST DIRTYWHORE CLAMDIGGER NASTYNYMPHO

 A "Sexy Word Challenge" dare using: THIGHS PRICKPRICKLE SPANKMEHARD BAGLICKER FILLALLMYHOLES PRISONWIFESWAP

 A "Video Recording" dare involving: WALKOFSHAME FILLALLYOURHOLES NIPPLETWEAKING RUMP CLAMJUICER CRAZEDCUNT

 A "Detail Nastiest Imaginable Masturbation Act Done By <person>" dare using: VARTING WRINKLEDBALLS BACK TONGUEMYTWAT RIMJOB COZYCUNT

 A "Draw/Write On Body" dare using: HOMEMADEHORSE SLAPTHATASS NIPPLETWEAKER HOTSPUNK CREAMPIEEATER ASSCRACK

Male Makes Up:

 An "Alternate Sexual Orientation" dare using: THIGH RUBSTERS THICKHARDDICK SLUTOMATIC ITSHUGE SEMENSUCKER

 An "Explicit Details For A Roleplay Scenario" dare inspired by: BEADEDBUTTPROBE PUSSYSLAPPING FACEFUCKER KNOB VARTING NICETITS

 A "Detail Sex In Wild Location" dare using: HUMILIATION SWINGERPARTY FUCKMYWIFE SLUTFUCKER ALLHOLESFILLED BALL

 An "Impersonate <person> Having Sex" dare inspired by: SLUMBERPARTY FUNBAGS FANNY PUSSYPISS QUICKFUCK JIZZINME

 An "Oral Pleasuring" dare inspired by: TRIPLEPENETRATION CUNTCREAM HYPNOTICORGASM YONI JIZZONMYBUTT FOOTJOB

 A "Draw/Write On Body" dare using: ANALINTERCOURSE HUMPMYLEG TASTESLIKEFISH ANALWINK PUSSYSLAP LEG

Female Makes Up:

 A "Foreplay Fun With Food" dare inspired by: SWEATYBALLS CUNTLEASH SCHOOLUNIFORM SLAPMYASS LICKMYCOCK CORNHUSKER

 A "Live Sex Demonstration" dare featuring: JILLJIZZ GIRLONGIRL HOMEMADEHORSE WIFESWAP LUSCIOUSLABIA LICKMYASS

 A "Self-Pleasuring" dare involving: DONKEYDILDO WILLYNILLY TIGHTTWATS GSPOTORGASM COLLARANDLEASH PEGMYBUTTHOLE

 A "Write Me A Love Note" dare using: EROTICSPANKING BALLSTRETCHER TABOOHOLE GREASEDPOLE TEASEMYTWAT HARDCOCK

 A "Draw/Write On Body" dare using: HUSBANDSHARING SUCCULENTSLIT SEXYBEAR CUNTCAGE SHALLOWTHRUST REBOUNDSEX

 A "Sex For Money" dare using: FUNBAGS BALLSTRETCHER BALLBITER JUNGLEFEVER SPANKMEHARD SLUMBERPARTY

Male Makes Up:

 A "Detail Nastiest Imaginable Masturbation Act Done By <person>" dare using: HOTSAUSAGE GLOBOFGOO GSPOTSPRAY SNOWBALLING NASTYNYMPHO BADGIRL

 An "Explicit Details For A Roleplay Scenario" dare inspired by: SHITHEAD TAUTTWAT DOGGYANAL LABIALICKING PUSSYPUDDING JUICYCUNT

 A "Crossdressing" dare inspired by: BLOWME FUCKMYPUSSYHARD BOOTLICKER WETPUSSY PUSHITIN WANKINGOFF

 A "Dark Fantasy Roleplay" dare using: SQUICK PERFECTPUSSY LABIASTRETCHER EDIBLEPASTIES GIANTANALDONG VIBRATINGPLUG

 A "Self-Pleasuring" dare involving: HUGEMONSTERCOCK MUFFDIVING SHORTDICK GSPOTGUSH SEMENSUCKERS COCKTEASE

 A "Draw/Write On Body" dare using: ASSNIBBLER HORNYSLUT SPREADERBAR PILLOWQUEEN NIPPLETWEAKER CREAMPIE

Substitute Truths

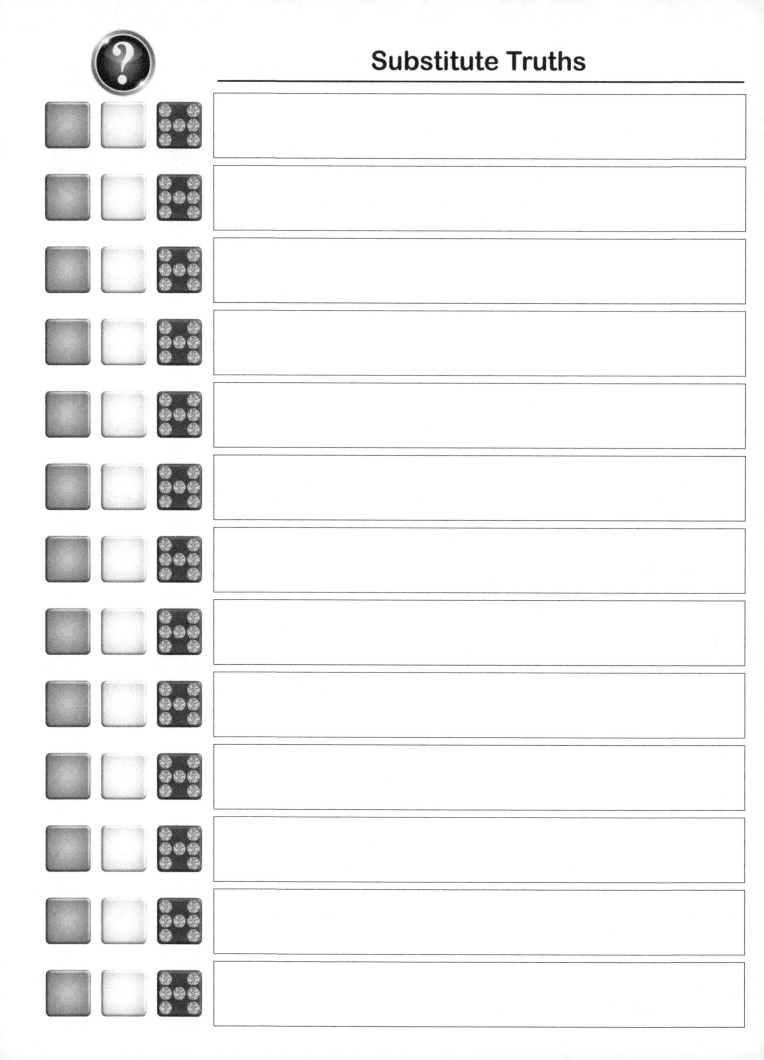

Substitute Dares

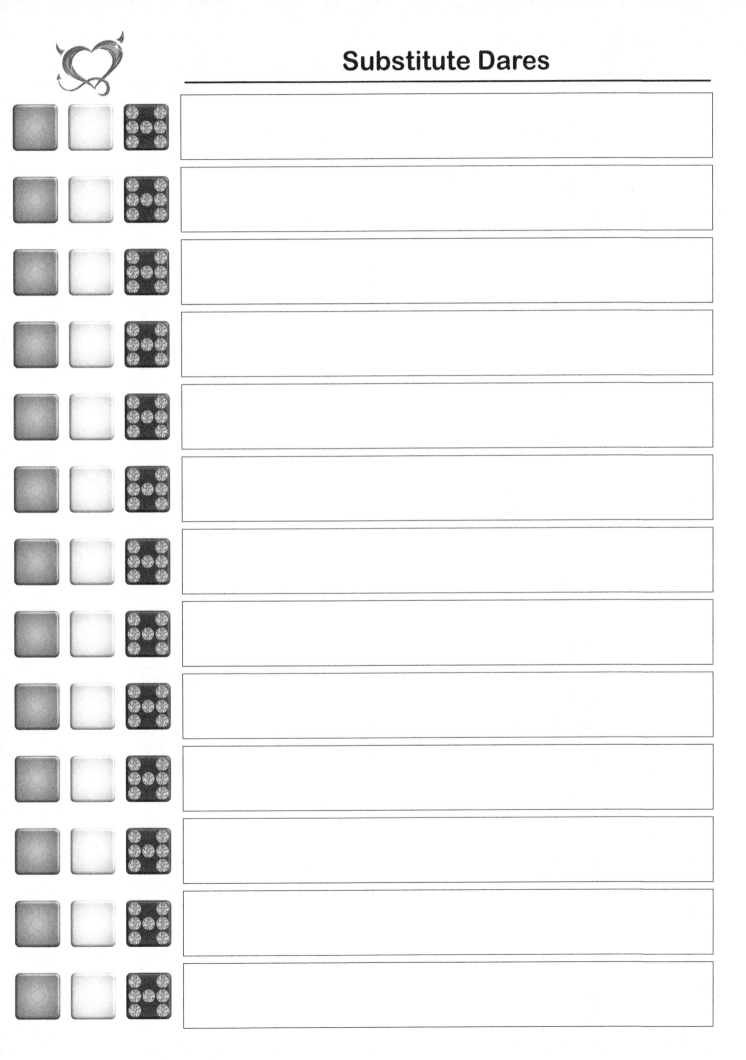

Substitute Truths

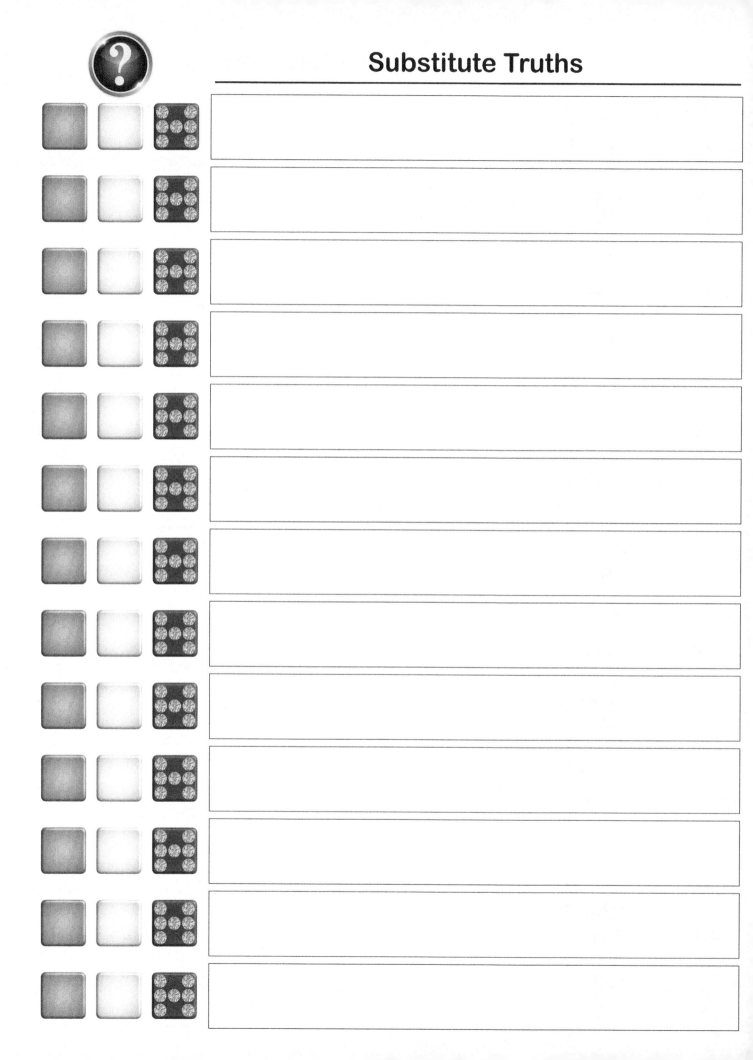

Substitute Dares

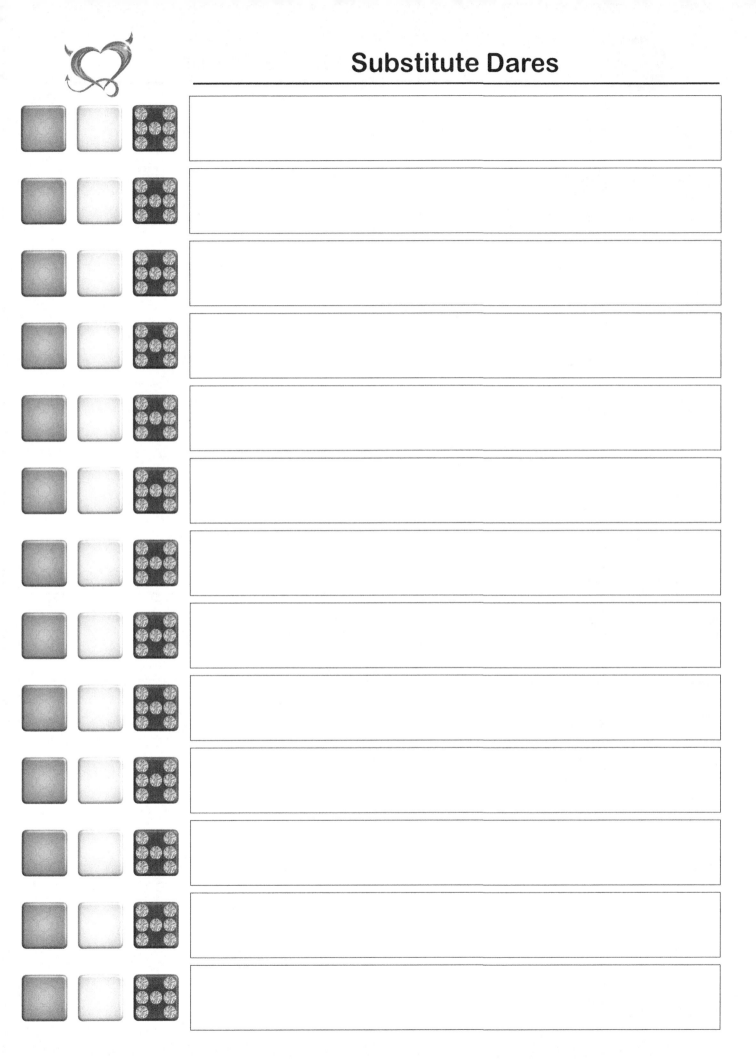

Substitute Truths

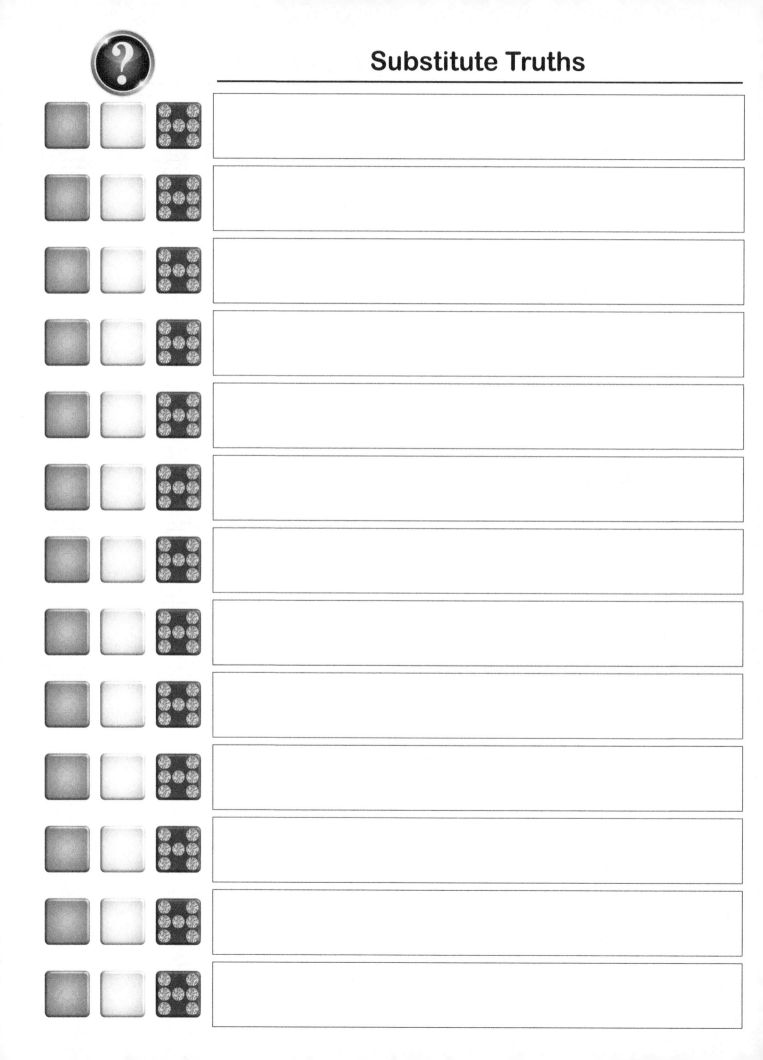

Substitute Dares

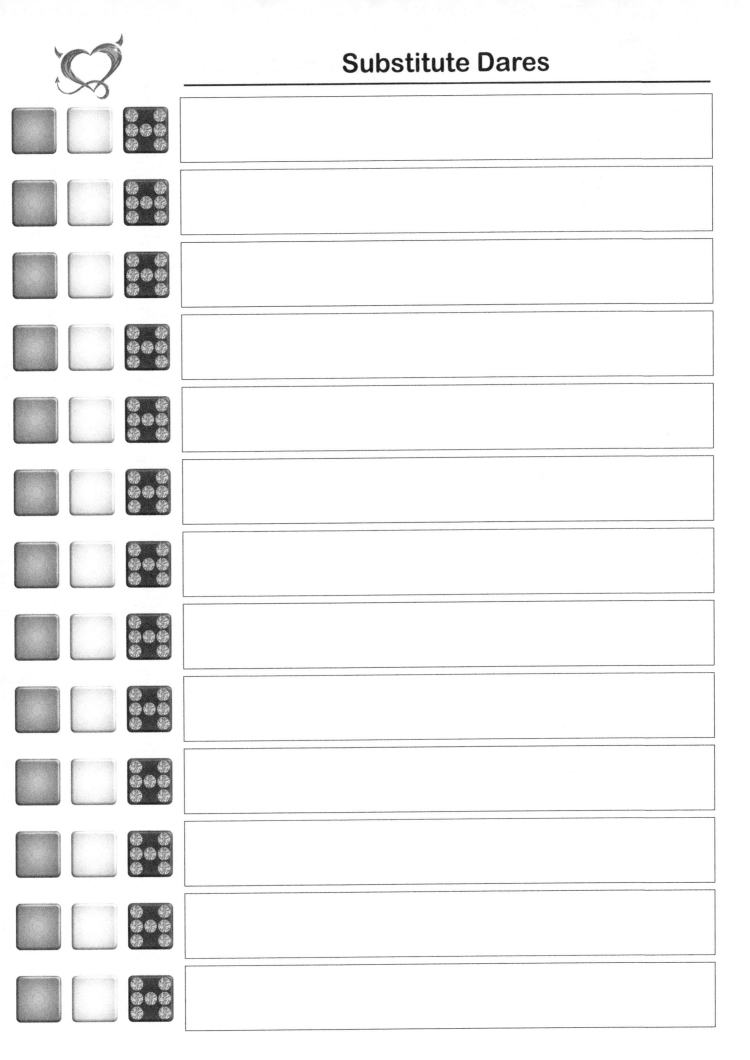

Substitute Truths

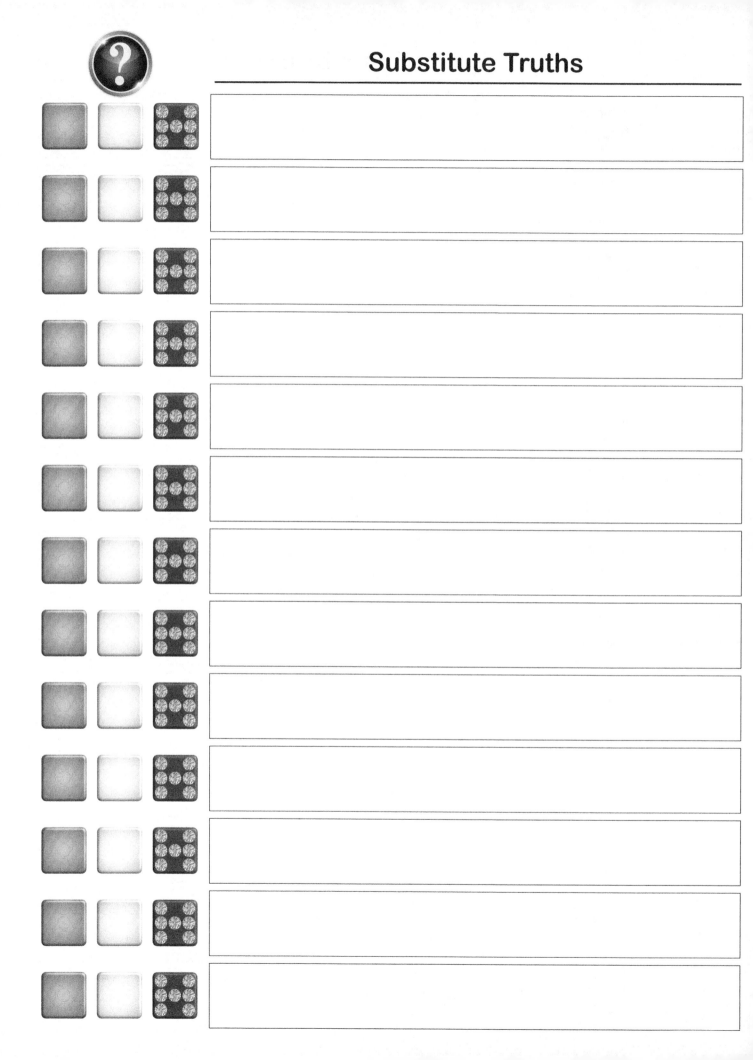

Substitute Dares

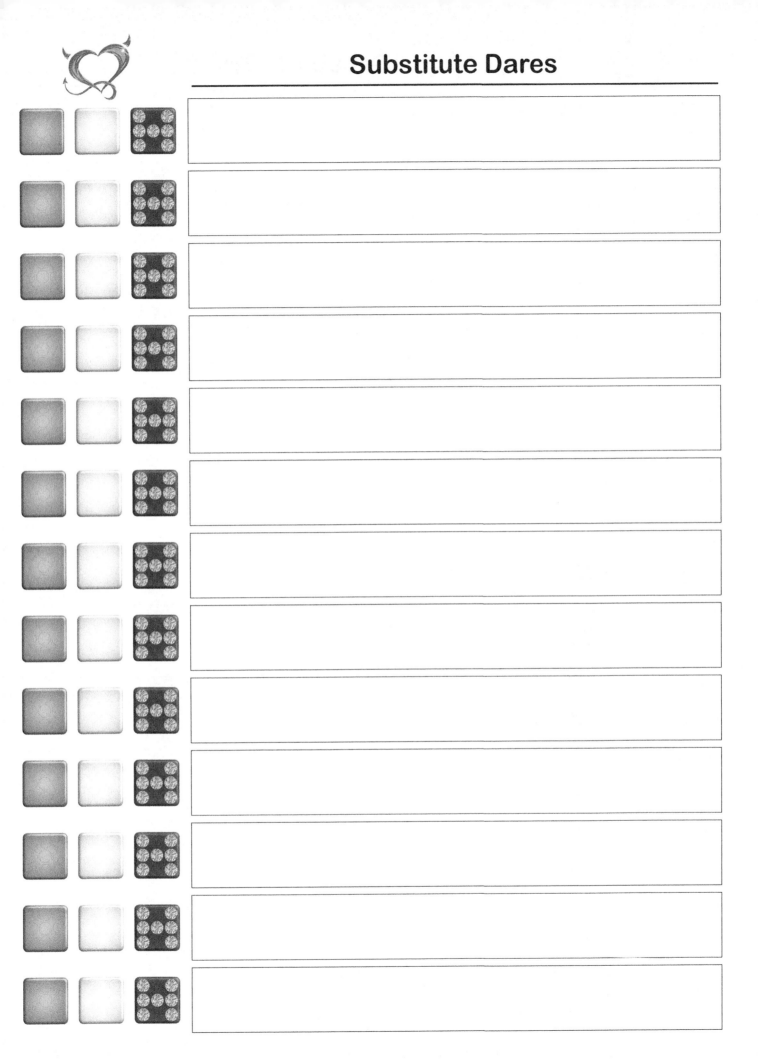

Substitute Truths

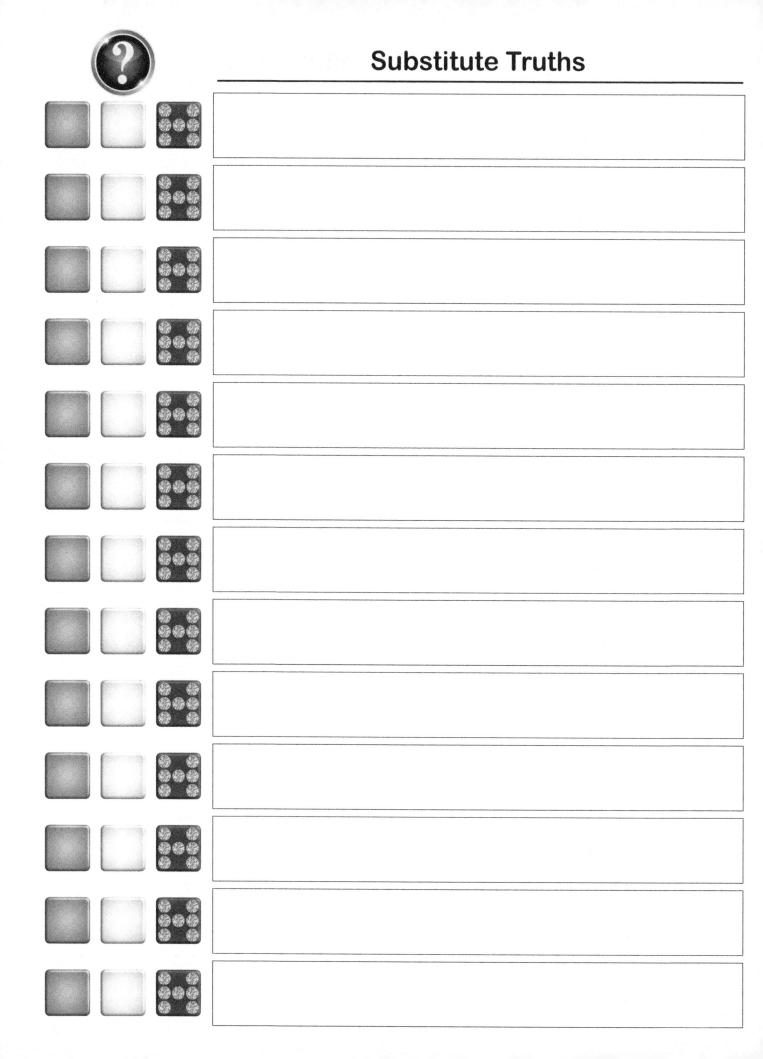

Substitute Dares

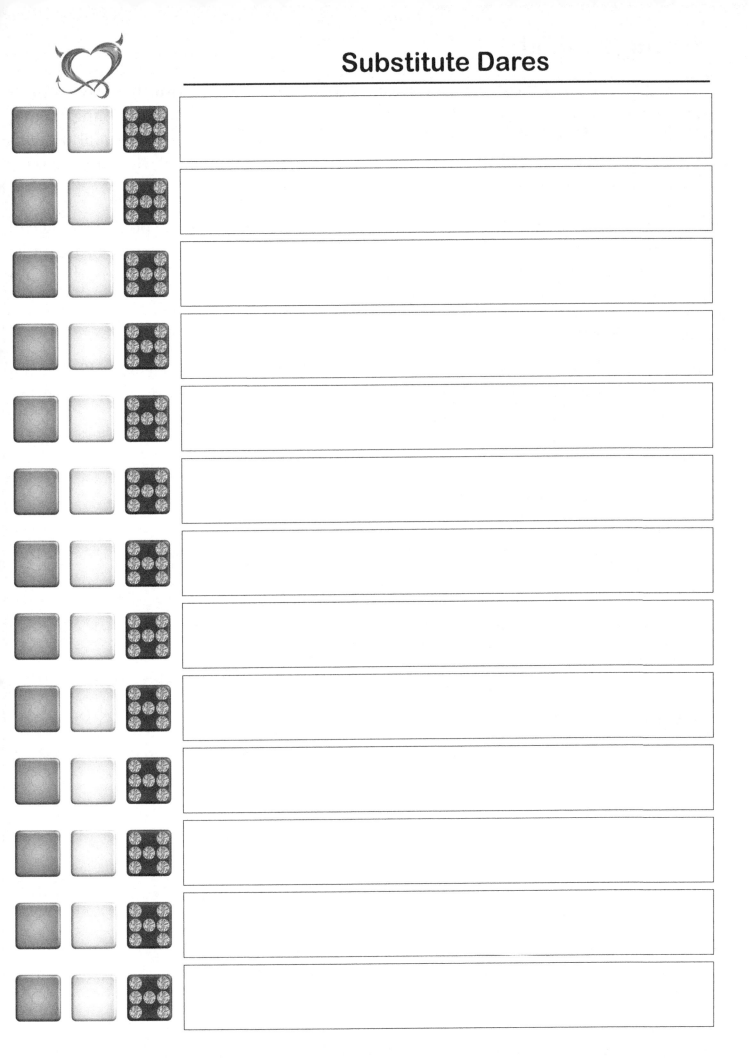

Fooling Around

Fooling Around is a dice-based game for couples to be played with the dirty truth or dare activities included in this book. The *tongue in cheek* design involves fooling around the Rim of a Hole. Deep inside the Hole are Hot Spots. Your goal is to fill the Hot Spots with your Pleasure Plugs. When the Hole is wholly plugged, the game is over. The winner is the player plugging the most hot spots.

Note: Two variations of the game "board" are the last pages of the book, so they can be torn out, played on and then stored with the book. Color PDF versions of the Hole design are available at: www.friskyforeplay.com/FoolingAround. The second version encourages more intimate, free style creativity.

How to Play

You will need 3 different colored dice (e.g., red, white, blue) and 6 Pleasure Plugs each (use coins, poker chips, etc.). The order and numbers on the three dice correspond to one of the stimulating ideas in the dirty truth or dare activity sets.

The game is relatively simple, but there are rules:

- Start with one Pleasure Plug each.

- Roll to determine starting player.

- Roll 3 dice every turn and move clockwise around the Rim using any single die.

- If you roll a double, you must attempt to enter the Hole - use one of the double dies.

- If you roll a triple, use one, two or three dice to move – Hole penetration optional.

- If you land on another plug, send it back to the Start.

- If you start in the Hole, you must reverse thrust and come back out of the Hole.

- When you end a move on a Hot Spot, it is considered Plugged - locked in place.

- When you plug a Hot Spot, start a new pleasure plug – all other players remove one item of clothing if they have any left on.

- When you land on a Frisky Spot (three dice icon), use all three dice to look up a dirty truth or dare for any target player. Cap the intensity level based on the number of plugged Hot Spots plus one (start at one and go up to six when 5 Hot Spots have been plugged).

- When you land on any other Pleasure Spot, perform the foreplay or gameplay activity indicated. The foreplay activities require your creative interpretation.

- Fooling Around ends when all the Hot Spots are plugged – Sex anyone?

- The winner is the player plugging the most Hot Spots. In a tie, the winner is the one who plugs the last Hot Spot.

Extra Details

Even simple games can become complicated so, here are a few extra details to ensure everyone plays for fun:

- Every player should have a distinctive type of Pleasure Plug so you can tell them apart and determine a winner.

- Each entry point can access two Hot Spots. You can move through and around unplugged Hot Spots, but if both Hot Spots are plugged, you must continue by moving back out of the Hole.

- While in the Hole, you can travel along any marked path in any available direction.

- Each player may have a maximum of 2 pleasure plugs in play (not yet locked in a Hot Spot). If you land on a location instructing you to start another plug but already have two in play, you must choose one of your plugs to move back to the start.

- If you have two pleasure plugs in play, you may move any token you desire. Also, in this situation, if you move one onto a Hot Spot, do not start another one yet.

- Players can take a shot if they can't or choose not to perform a dare or answer a sex question.

- There are 8 special icons used on the circular pleasure spots:

 **Frisky Spot**: choose a target player then lookup a truth or dare in the activity booklet corresponding to the dice rolled. Cap the intensity level to one plus the number of Hot Spots plugged.

 **Sensual Lips**: Perform an oral pleasuring activity for your lover. Kiss, lick and suck on one of the body parts identified on the pleasure spot.

 Romantic Intimacy: Perform a pleasuring activity that is tender and loving as indicated. Explore intimate and sensual feelings.

 **Looks Hot**: These pleasure spots are intended for you to provide visual stimulation for your lover as indicated. Creatively pleasure yourself as well.

 Liquid Courage: Everyone takes a nice sip of a drink to help loosen inhibitions and lubricate your kinky desires.

Naughty Dares: These devilish icons are purposely placed around the Hole. These are similar to Frisky Spots but only dares are selected for the target player using the dice roll.

 Carnal Knowledge: These are similar to Frisky Spots but only dirty questions are selected for the target player using the dice roll.

 Hot Spots: The flaming hearts indicate locations to lock in your pleasuring plugs.

Note: with three or more people playing, the current player can choose any other player to participate in an activity. However, when landing on the Frisky Spot, Naughty Dares or Carnal Knowledge spots, you could have all other players roll to determine the participant. Or, go wild and have all other players get involved in sequence. Use either the top or bottom activity sets as appropriate. Slight changes to the wording may be required. You could do the same for the other game locations as well.

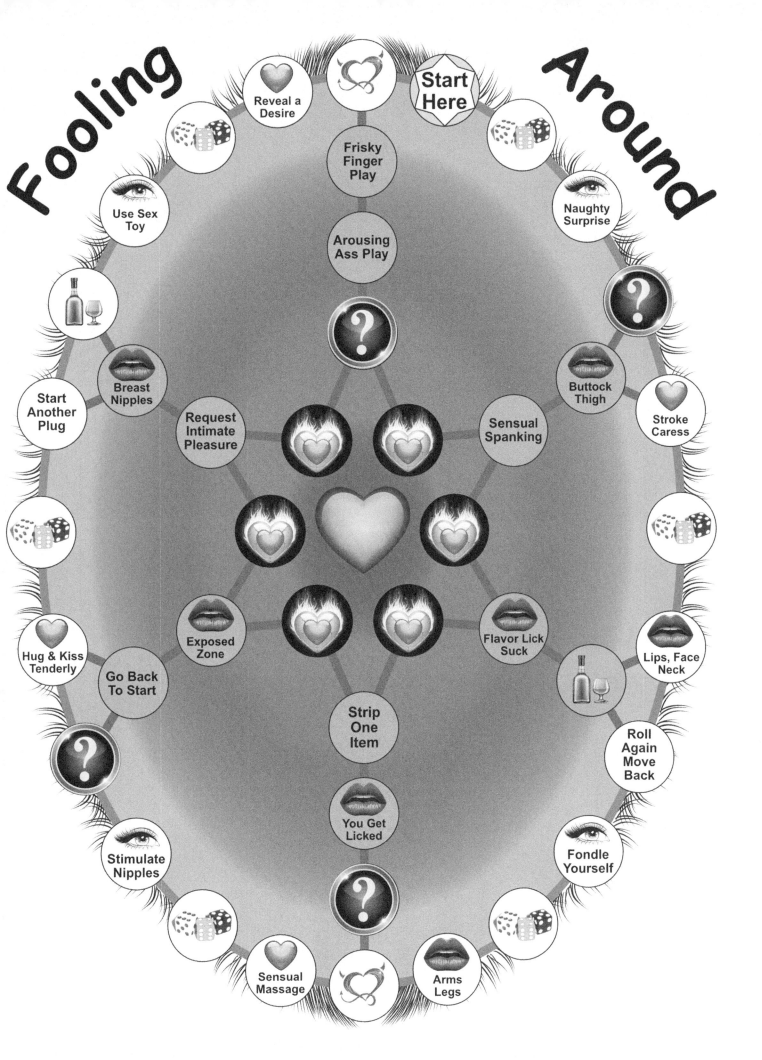

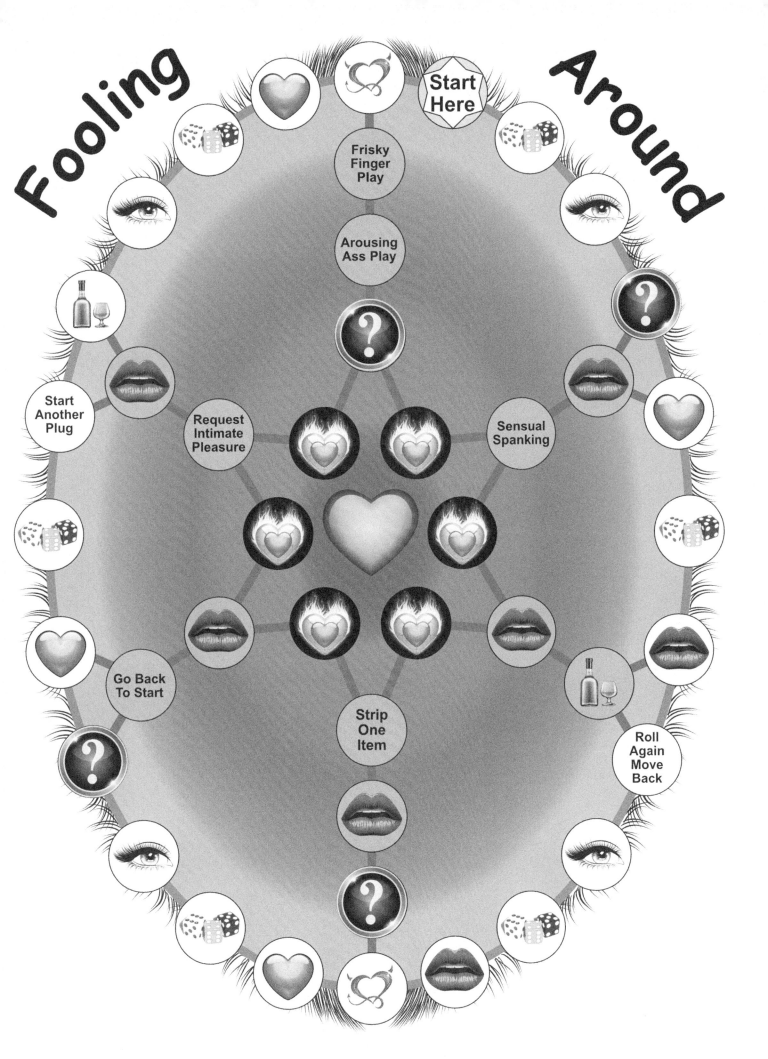